THE LAWYER'S GUIDE TO
Summation®

Tom O'Connor

LawPracticeManagementSection
MARKETING • MANAGEMENT • TECHNOLOGY • FINANCE

Commitment to Quality: The Law Practice Management Section is committed to quality in our publications. Our authors are experienced practitioners in their fields. Prior to publication, the contents of all our books are rigorously reviewed by experts to ensure the highest quality product and presentation. Because we are committed to serving our readers' needs, we welcome your feedback on how we can improve future editions of this book.

This publication was made possible with the generous financial support of Summation Legal Technologies, Inc., developer of Summation® software. No endorsement of the products or services of this company should be inferred by their support.

Cover design by Jim Colao.

Library of Congress Cataloging-in-Publication Data
The Lawyer's Guide to Summation®. Tom O'Connor. Library of Congress Cataloging-in-Publication Data is on file.

ISBN 1-59031-383-6

08 07 06 05 04   5 4 3 2 1

Discounts are available for books ordered in bulk. Special consideration is given to state bars, CLE programs, and other bar-related organizations. Inquire at Book Publishing, American Bar Association, 321 N. Clark Street, Chicago, Illinois 60610.

Contents

PART II
Popular Features

CHAPTER 5
Transcripts

CHAPTER 6
OCR Base

CHAPTER 7
Electronic Evidence

CHAPTER 8
Orchestrating Your Case

PART III
Using Summation

CHAPTER 9
Using Summation in Your Practice

About the Author

Tom O'Connor is a nationally known consultant, speaker, and writer in the area of computerized litigation support systems. He is a New England native who graduated from the Johns Hopkins University in 1972 with a B.A. in Political Science. After attending law school for one year at the University of Notre Dame, Tom returned to Baltimore and undertook a career as a paralegal specializing in complex litigation.

His initial exposure to a document-intensive case came several years later when he assisted several public interest firms in Boston with a class-action voting rights suit brought on behalf of patients at state hospitals. Over the years he has been involved in asbestos litigation, the Keating case, the San Diego Civic Center construction litigation, California class actions against crematoriums, national breast implant litigation, tobacco litigation on behalf of the Attorney General of Texas, and various phases of the Enron litigation.

Tom's involvement with large cases led him to become familiar with dozens of various software applications for litigation support, and he has both designed databases and trained legal staffs in their use on many of the cases mentioned above. This work has involved both public and private law firms of all sizes across the nation and, over the past several years, has expanded to include electronic document depositories and trial presentation systems.

A frequent lecturer on the subject of legal technology, Tom has been on the faculty of numerous national CLE providers and currently teaches a course on legal technology in an ABA-approved paralegal program at a local college. He is also a member of the planning board for the annual ABA TECHSHOW® as well as the advisory board of the national LegalTech conferences. A prolific writer on legal technology, Tom is also the author of *The*

Automated Law Firm, a guide to computer systems and software published by Aspen Law & Business, now in its fourth edition.

Tom resides in the Puget Sound area with his fifteen-year-old son, Seamus. They hope someday to have their own float in the Krewe of Tucks Mardi Gras parade in which they ride every year, down the Mississippi in New Orleans.

Acknowledgments

I would like to acknowledge the assistance of Beverly Loder, whose patience and persistence made the completion of this project possible; Bil Kellermann of Summation, whose knowledge and cooperation were essential to the technical accuracy of the content (some of which he graciously provided); and Kevin Craft of Pacific Legal, for being such a good friend.

As always, nothing I do would be possible without the companionship of Gayle, who showed me how to live again one day at a time, and Seamus, who shows me every day how much fun that can be.

Winning Cases with Summation

Foreword by Jon Sigerman
President, Summation Legal Technologies, Inc.

In 1982 David Rotman and I conceived the idea for what became Summation. At the time David was a megafirm litigation partner and I was a solo practitioner. Really, we combined our ideas for applying personal computers to litigation support.

I had a large docket of smaller cases, some of which at any given time were hot, while others were not. My desire was to have a system that made it easy for me to winnow each case down to a critical mass of evidence by clipping and assimilating excerpts of the key portions of documents or deposition transcripts. Then I wanted to be able to easily retrieve, by case, a digital representation of the essence of the case ordered in a meaningful way—either chronologically, by a hierarchical outline, or in the order that best conveyed the case theme.

David, on the other hand, wanted a platform on his and his paralegal's desktop IBM PCs to index and archive the potentially important documents and transcripts from a case. His goal was to search and retrieve document summaries or transcript testimony. (As an outside counsel for IBM, he was able to obtain one of the first-production-run IBM PCs).

Both of us wanted to edit summaries and make notes about important transcript excerpts. And we both wanted to be able to do it ourselves—use our keyboards to retrieve and apply our thoughts to the information.

Working with a third founder, system engineer James Henderson, we set out to develop a system to store disparate types of evidence (transcripts, document abstracts, and thought annotations), compartmentalized by case, into one software program. That program had to be simple enough for nonprogrammers like us to use, allowing us to one-stop search, annotate, and mark what was important. After many Sunday nights (we all had full-time jobs or practices, so our project efforts were restricted to Sunday), and a few misfires along the way, we publicly released our first integrated transcript-management and document-control-and-retrieval product in 1988.

With an early version of Summation on a laptop computer, I was able to walk around the site of an incident and review the depositions as I retraced the alleged events. This allowed me to find physical proof to establish an unequivocal contradiction—I could prove the plaintiff lied in deposition. I was also able to use Summation on my laptop at a court trial podium.

In one memorable instance, in response to an unanticipated question raised by the judge in a multimillion-dollar case, I did a quick search and found a responsive trial exhibit abstract and image. The document had not previously been on the collective case radar for the issue posed by the judge's question. The opposition responded first, and flailed at the question. When I got the nod, I simply directed court to a region of the document. The judge's findings accompanying judgment in favor of my client explicitly cited the document passage.

Summation's notion of an integrated litigation support system has progressed over many product generations. New types of sources of case information have been integrated into our software—images, e-mail, Microsoft Word files, PDF files, and more. And as Summation became a standard litigation tool, the system has taken major leaps from a closed-form single-user system for an individual lawyer to a collaborative network system. We continued to develop our stand-alone systems for solo practitioners like me when I started Summation, and for smaller intrafirm fiefdoms like David's labor litigation group. But we also took the leap to develop a collaborative network system. Our network system consists of a "mother ship" central server that can be populated by coding, imaging, and other stage-setting workstations. This central server can be accessed by end users on a litigation team. Even multiple litigation teams representing multiple parties in different locales with a commonality of interest (such as codefendants or plaintiffs assigned to a multidistrict litigation panel) can access the central system.

Not only did we create network and standalone systems, but we developed combinations of the two. Our central network server system can populate a notebook computer with information in places where no network connection is available, such as a courtroom, opponent's conference room, or airplane. An entire case or portions of a case can be easily delivered *en masse* to the notebook. We also extended our network system to a Web server that can be accessed with an Internet browser. Information for our notebook computer application can be populated from the Web server when a connection is available, and then be used by a road warrior where no Internet or network connection is available. This notebook system creates a personal "key case information" disaster-recovery system. Ultimately, we embarked upon a mega-case client server version by taking advantage of Microsoft's versatile SQL Server 2000 engine.

Summation covers a broad spectrum of critical litigation functions for a wide variety of the litigation marketplace, which is probably why we perennially win the major industry awards. This breadth of functional variety and flexibility is often misunderstood, which is why Summation is sometimes referred to as a complex system. The fact of the matter is that litigation *is* complex, and as such our litigation tool needs to be crafted to handle the range of complexities inherent in the litigation process. But don't be misled—Summation can be simple. One of the great aspects of this book is that it nicely highlights Summation's simplicity; it identifies certain functions from Summation's entire integrated litigation-support product line that give great value to a lawyer in any size or any type of case, yet require little learning investment. These include several of our products' most-used functions:

- ◆ Searching from within a transcript, and making virtual "sticky notes" as the transcript is reviewed
- ◆ Searching from within a document collection grid, and reordering the list of documents by simple sorting
- ◆ The multitranscript Case Explorer search, which reveals common words or phrases used by witnesses in the entire testimonial record
- ◆ The integrated "one-stop" Case Explorer search, which allows all types and sources of information possibly germane to a case to be searched with a unified command, and displayed in a unified report

You can master each of these simple functions in minutes. A lawyer or paralegal can derive incredible value from learning these functions, without ever having to get much deeper into the system.

This book also breaks down how to use Summation from start to finish—from case intake to case resolution by motion or trial. Regardless of the complexity of the case, or the number of Summation features used, the same steps are followed:

- ◆ Information is used to create a Summation case
- ◆ Once the information is loaded into a case, it is made available in whole or part to authorized end users from the single point of access that Summation provides
- ◆ The information that does not meet a threshold level of significance is segregated (or made severable) from the central case repository

After following these steps, a lawyer then has the technological tools to take command of the evidence. Our product mantra is "command over the evidence wins cases."

Introduction

The purpose of this book is to give lawyers and paralegals a quick overview of how Summation works. It assumes that the reader has already purchased Summation and has had a basic introduction to its general functions or, as is more typical, has been shown how to use a specific feature for the management of some evidentiary material in an ongoing piece of litigation. That first exposure to Summation has now raised questions about how to use the program in a more comprehensive manner.

This may seem to beg the question "Why use Summation at all?" As Jon Sigerman points out in the foreword to this book, the underlying reason is that Summation provides an integrated litigation support system that offers one platform for organizing a wide variety of case information. Indeed, Summation was the original integrated litigation support product, although when it was first introduced, the term *integration* meant only a way to simultaneously search the full text of deposition transcripts and a database index of deposition exhibits. Now, as Jon further points out, the range of evidence extends from traditional transcripts and exhibits to electronic documents that may be text, images, or even e-mail with accompanying metadata.

To show how Summation can be used to manage this wide variety of material, I have organized this book from the perspective of actually working with evidentiary documents. There are two general categories of Summation features. Part 1 of this book, "Core Features" (Chapters 1 to 4), shows the basic Summation structure for beginning a case, organizing evidence, and searching through that evidence. Part 2, "Popular Features" (Chapters 5 to 8), discusses the tools that those at Summation have found are most commonly used for handling specific types of material. Part 3, "Using Summation," covers the Summation tasks that accompany each activity in a case, from case intake to post-trial documents.

At various points in the text, you will find sidebars called "Practice Pointers" that discuss how a certain Summation feature differs from a more traditional approach to organizing evidence. These are designed to illustrate a new paradigm or process that Summation uses to make the task of managing litigation more efficient through computer technology. Choosing which of these is most useful to you in your case is the key to making Summation work for you.

Read this book for an overview of all the tools that Summation offers, then use the ones that are best for you on any specific case. The features you use may in fact differ from case to case. Readers who have heard me speak at legal technology conferences around the country know that I believe it is this sort of flexibility that makes a legal software application truly effective.

Core Features

Opening a Case

Opening a case in Summation is an easy task. After you click on the **Summation** icon on your desktop to open the program, the first screen you are presented with after the "welcome" window looks like Figure 1.

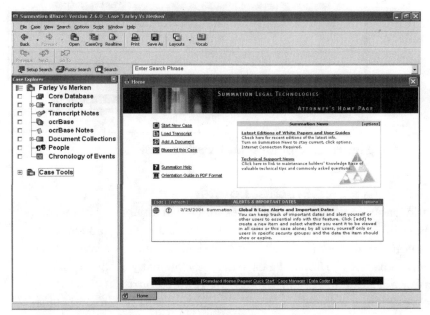

Figure 1. Summation's Home Page.

This screen may be customized to show other views or layouts. This particular layout, with the home page content on the right and the traditional Explorer-type interface on the left, is called the ***docked explorer layout*** (the case shown here is a demo case that comes already loaded in Summation). You can choose from a variety of layouts; the one you choose will be specific to you, even if you are working in a network environment.

Start by clicking on the **Case** menu near the top of the window and then select **New** to start a new case or, as illustrated below, select **Open** to choose an existing case (see Figure 2).

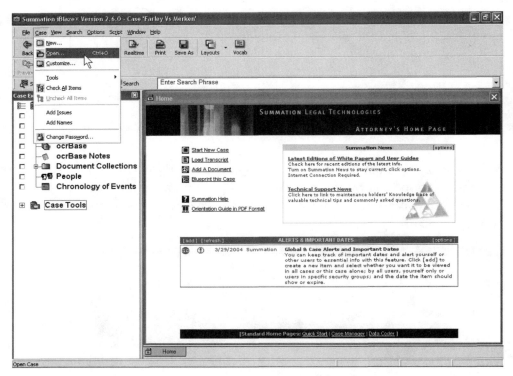

Figure 2. Opening an Existing Case.

Practice Pointer

In the traditional law firm, case files may be in any one of numerous locations: a file room, a lawyer's office, a paralegal's desk, a secretarial station, a conference room, or a library. Worse still from an organizational standpoint, separate portions of a case file may be in any of those various locations or even outside the firm at a copy center, courthouse, or someone's home. Finding a specific item can be problematic and losing something is inevitable.

With Summation, all of your cases and all of their components are in one location, easily accessible by everyone in the firm who needs them. Originals are never lost, copies are never misfiled, and an overview of all work product can be conducted by one person at a desk, not numerous people searching all over the firm, and in seconds, not hours.

The case list then appears in a separate box (see Figure 3). Double-click on the case you wish to open, or click once on the case and then click **Select**.

You can also access a list of the most recently opened cases. Simply click on the **File** menu and the six most recently opened cases will be listed at the bottom of the pop-up box.

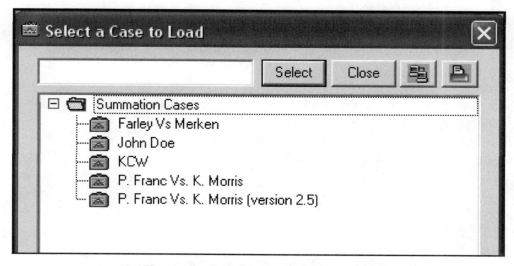

Figure 3. Selecting a Case to Load.

The Case Explorer

2

The Case Explorer tree is on the left side of the screen in the docked explorer view and is divided into two working sections (see Figure 4 on page 9). The upper section is under the case name heading (**Farley Vs Merken**, in this example), and contains a series of elements that are shared by all users who have access to this specific case. The lower section, under the **Case Tools**

Practice Pointer

The Case Explorer is the electronic organizer for your case. It not only replaces the filing cabinet full of redwells and bookshelves of binders in your office, it also allows you to instantly view the contents of an entire case, something that is impossible with paper files.

Furthermore, you can customize the way you look at the case by making subfolders to share document collections, important people, facts, notes you have made as you review documents, and even case chronologies. In addition, you can make your own personalized folders for organizing documents around your own thoughts on the case, saved searches to be reused as new documents come in, slideshows of documents you feel are important, and various views and layouts to "slice" the data in ways you feel are important—all without changing the way other staff members look at the original documents.

heading, contains folders and tools that are personal to each individual user. To see the list of tools, click on the box to the left of the **Case Tools** heading.

The Case Explorer may be customized by using drag-and-drop on items to rearrange them. In addition, display options such as font style, color, and size may be adjusted.

Folders may be added, deleted, or grouped together, with the exception that a shared item cannot be moved to the personal folders area and vice versa.

By default, Summation provides a standard set of elements for each case. By simply right-clicking on the case name and choosing **Create New,** the following types of folders may be added to the searchable, shared area of the Case Explorer:

- ◆ Transcript Groups
- ◆ Saved Searches Folders
- ◆ Document Collections Folders
- ◆ eDocs and eMail Folders
- ◆ Pleadings Folders
- ◆ Slideshow Folders
- ◆ Layouts Folders
- ◆ Scripts Folders
- ◆ Repositories for Remote Transcripts and Documents
- ◆ Repositories for Companion Documents

In the same manner, the following types of folders can be added to the Case Tools (or personal) area of the Case Explorer:

- ◆ Scripts Folders
- ◆ Saved Searches Folders
- ◆ Slideshow Folders

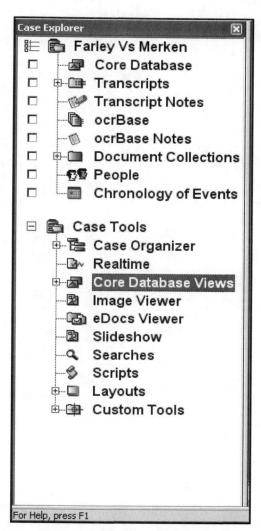

Figure 4. The Case Explorer Tree.

Organizing Your Evidence

3

Transcripts

Full-text versions of the transcripts of depositions, hearings, or trials may be obtained from court reporters and loaded into Summation in order to allow searches for key words or phrases. The process of loading transcripts is fairly straightforward and is accomplished by clicking on the **File** menu and selecting **Load Transcript** (see Figure 5). A simple pop-up menu walks you through the process.

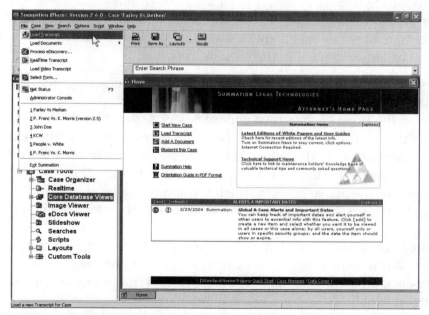

Figure 5. Selecting "Load Transcript."

Once transcripts have been loaded, there are two other functions in addition to word and phrase searches that may be of value. The first of these is the software equivalent of the traditional page and line summary, which Summation calls *digesting.* The second is the ability to add electronic comments or notes to the text of the transcript.

Practice Pointer

With paper transcripts, you read through the text and use a highlighter or colored "sticky note" to mark sections of importance. Summation allows you to search the transcript for words or phrases far faster than you can read it, and then take the specific lines you find and copy them to another Summation file for later searching, or to a word processor for use in a memo or brief.

Not only do you save time by not reading every page, but you don't have to return to the original, make copies, or spend time dictating a summary. You quickly and easily create a new file on the computer that you can then just as quickly retrieve and use whenever you need it.

Digest Files

Digests are text files that contain excerpts from transcripts. As such, they can be opened by a word processor (simply right-click to select an excerpt to move by copying to the clipboard), or searched in the same manner as a transcript (see Chapter 4). Please note, however, that digest files cannot be placed in the Case Explorer tree; they can only be retrieved using the **Digest** menu.

A digest file can be created in the following manner:

1. Open the transcript you wish to digest or, if you are digesting multiple transcripts, open the first one.
2. Click on the **Digest** menu, then choose **Select Active Digest File**.
3. To create a new digest file, enter the name of the new file in the text box at the bottom of the **Select Active Digest File** dialog and click on **Select.** If you are using an existing digest file, select it from the list. This is now the active file into which testimony will be copied.
4. Scroll to the first area of testimony you wish to copy into the digest file.
5. Highlight the lines of testimony to be copied by holding the left mouse button down while dragging the cursor down over the lines of text.
6. Right-click on the highlighted area and select **Write to digest "[name of digest file]."**
7. Continue this process for each excerpt you wish to add to the digest file.

Notes

Unlike digests, which are static text files that exist outside of Summation, notes are reusable summaries, comments, or annotations that exist in the transcript itself. Notes can be added to a transcript at any time while it is open in Summation. When you create a note, a small icon appears in the left margin of the transcript to indicate a note is attached to that line. Clicking on the icon opens the note. (Figure 6 illustrates a note.)

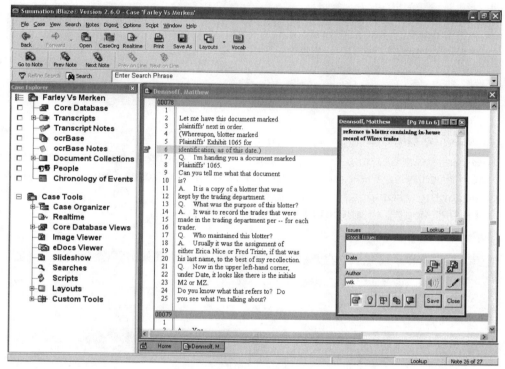

Figure 6. Transcript Note.

To add a new note:

1. Open a transcript and scroll to the line of testimony where you wish to add a note.
2. Move your cursor to the far left margin past the pleading line numbers. When the cursor changes to a pointing finger, double-click the left mouse button. (If a note already exists on this line, you may add a second note but you must use the **Notes** menu and select **Add Note**.)
3. Type your comments into the body of the note. You may also enter information into the Issues, Date, and Author fields. Use the icons at the bottom of the note box to select a note type or to attach images or audio files.
4. Click **Save** as you create the note to keep your comments while leaving the note open for additional text.

5. Click **Close** to close the note. (You will be prompted to save any changes you have made, but there is an option in the **Close** dialog that allows automatic saving without this prompt.)[1]

Practice Pointer

Your own individual comments are added directly to the transcript as an electronic note and can be reviewed by anyone browsing through the transcript, or searched and reviewed independently. Here again, you are not required to carry around a paper transcript marked with yellow tags or paper clips. And unlike hard copies, these electronic notes can be sorted by issues and immediately retrieved by a specific issue you wish to review.

Rapid-Fire Digesting

There is a way to combine the functions of excerpting a digest and creating notes by copying the excerpts directly into the text area of a note. Simply highlight the testimony to excerpt, right-click your mouse (or press [CTRL+D]) and select **Copy Excerpt into New Note** (see Figure 7).

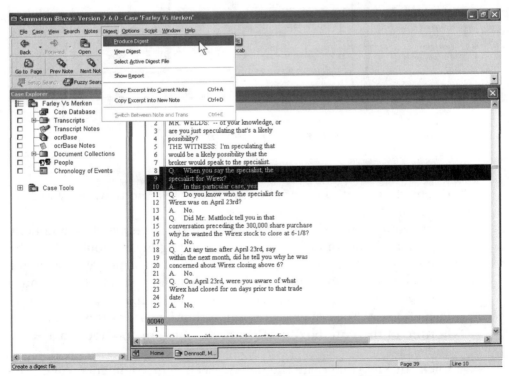

Figure 7. Copying an Excerpt into a Note.

If you use the auto-save feature for notes as mentioned above and use the keystroke combination of [CTRL+D] when you highlight the excerpt, you can quickly move through the transcript, excerpting relevant testimony as you move down the page. This combination is referred to as ***rapid-fire digesting.*** The benefit is that you can quickly move through transcripts and grabbing key pieces of testimony into notes. Please be aware, however, that no enhancements are made to the note fields using this technique. If you want to add information such as issues and dates to the notes, you will have to do this at a later time.[2]

The Core Database

Information about evidentiary documents is added to the Core Database in Summation by filling out a form with fields for information such as author, date, document number, document type, and so on. The standard form used in Summation for this process looks like the form shown in Figure 8.

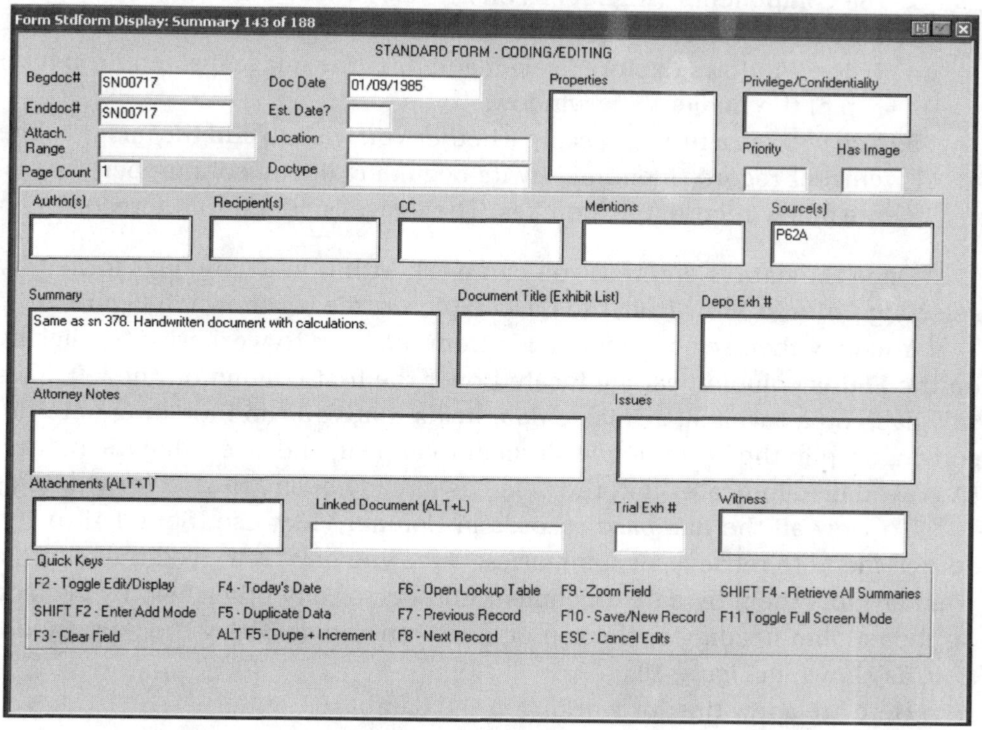

Figure 8. The Core Database Coding/Editing Window.

The actual entering of this information is often referred to as ***coding.*** It may be done directly by you or you may engage an outside vendor specializing in this type of data entry. If you perform this function, data is entered or coded one document at a time. If a vendor does the coding, that vendor provides you with all the data in a file called a ***load file*** that automatically performs a batch entry of all the data into your database.

If you wish to scan paper documents to create electronic pictures or images of the documents, it is relatively easy to link those images to the database records using standard drag-and-drop functionality.[3]

To add an image to a database record, first open both the database and Windows Explorer. Then do the following:

1. Open the database in Column View and scroll to the record you wish to link to an image. (There needs to be a bolded box around any one of the fields in this record. If there is no box appearing around one of the fields in the record, click once on the record to make the bolding appear.)
2. Open the Image View by double-clicking on **Image** in the Case Explorer Case Tools.
3. If you wish, dock or float the Image View to make it easier to work with the components. (Right-click on the **Image View** title bar and select either **Dock View → Right** or **Float View**.)
4. Using Windows Explorer, select and drag the image file and drop it on top of the **Image View** window.
5. You will see a prompt asking whether you wish to add the image to the current record (identified by its beginning document number) or create a new record. Click on **Yes.** The image is added to the record.

Once the data is entered, you can work with it in a columnar format by selecting **Column View** from the Case Explorer tree, as shown in Figure 9.

You may then select which fields from the form to work with by clicking on the **Fields** column heading located over the first column on the left. This will give you a list of all available data fields that you can then drag onto the screen, drop in the order you wish them to appear, and size using the mouse. (A grayed field indicates that the field has already been selected for viewing.)

To view all the database records in Column View, use [Shift+F4] or the **Search** menu to retrieve all summaries. Once you have retrieved the records, you may sort them by date, document number, or any other field by clicking on the column heading at the top of a column and selecting the **Sort By** option, as shown in Figure 10.

Here are a few tips for working in the database:

◆ You can resize the Form, Column, or Image views individually by dragging the edges of the window. However, the Query window is fixed in size and cannot be resized.
◆ If you have linked images to your database records, remember to open the Image View in order to see the images. As you select a document

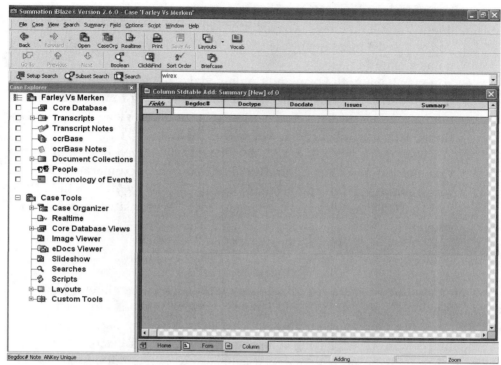

Figure 9. Viewing Data in Column View.

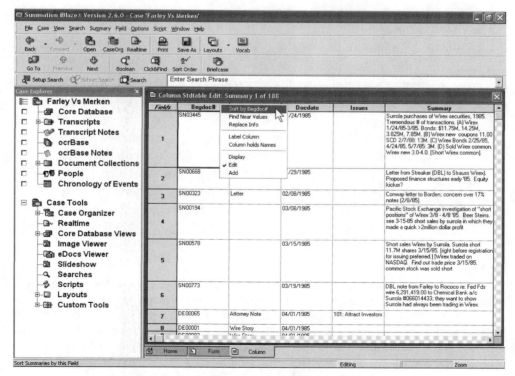

Figure 10. Sorting Database Records.

in Column or Form View, the image(s) for that document appear in Image View. If no image is associated with the selected document, then you will see a message in the Image View window stating that there is no associated image.

◆ You may have both Form and Column views open, but they operate independently. To synchronize them so that moving to a record in Column View brings the same summary up in Form View, go to the **Options** menu and select **Sync Form & Columns.**

◆ You may mark records in Column View by moving your cursor to the extreme left and clicking on the field number. Once marked, click on the **Summary** menu and select **Marking Options,** which include OCR, saving to PDF format, and marking as a HotFact for later search and retrieval.

Practice Pointer

Case documents have traditionally been copied, then indexed by a clerk or paralegal and stored in binders or filing cabinets. Retrieving a document meant searching through the index, determining where the document was stored, having someone retrieve it, making another copy (which you might put in a binder of your own with yet another index of your own "hot docs") and then returning it to the storage location. Of course, if someone else had the document or had misfiled it, you would have to go through the entire process again with the originals.

With Summation, the index is electronic and can be searched with your computer by any number of criteria that you set when the index is created. If you imaged the original documents instead of copying them, you can immediately bring up an electronic image of the original on your computer screen to review. From there, you can add comments to the document index, instantly make an electronic copy, and move it to your own issue organizer or case timeline in Summation. You can even send it to someone else for review in an e-mail message, or save it as an HTML document. And if you need a quick hard copy to give someone, simply hit the **Print** button.

Notes

1. You can also use the **Options** menu and select **Defaults**, click on the **Notes** tab, deselect **Prompt to Save on Close**, and select **Auto Close on Excerpt**.

2. Comparison of Find Note and Digest functionality: A digest can be very similar in function to the Find Note operation. Using both tools, you can create a report based on issues within the transcripts. The primary difference is the output. Using Find Note will display only the contents to only those notes created by an individual or containing a partic-

ular date. The report created by the Find Note feature is intended to produce a quick and easy report of all notes based solely on issue-coding or on the rapid-fire copy-and-paste results. You can also easily import the digest file into a word-processing document. When you create a digest, the highlighted testimony is only preserved in the digest itself. There is no evidence of the segments that were "digested" in the transcript itself. Excerpting transcript testimony into a note, however, preserves the excerpt for future reference in the transcript. Transcript notes can also be selected as a search item in the Case Explorer. Finally, notes can be organized by page and line reference, date, or issue. The digest is organized in the order in which the information is captured (rapid-fire digest) or alphabetically by issue using the single- or all-issue digest format.

3. Please note that the process described above typically involves a relatively low number of documents and assumes that you are familiar with current scanning technology. Most litigation support vendors who provide coding services will actually scan the documents first and then have data entry clerks code directly from the images by using either large monitors or dual monitors with the Summation form and the document image side by side. They then provide you with a load file that allows batch entry of both the database records and the images linked to those records.

Searching Your Evidence

4

General Tools

There are several tools available from the home page screen for performing simple searches. These include Quick Search, Fuzzy Search, and Vocabulary. (Figure 11 shows the results of searching transcript notes.)

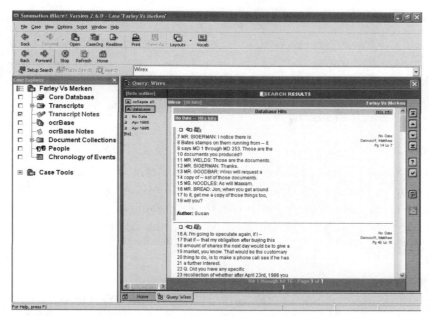

Figure 11. Transcript Notes Search Results.

Practice Pointer

You want to find out if a certain name appears in your discovery documents. How do you do that with paper? You start looking through the document, one page at a time. With Summation, you are offered a variety of electronic search tools that not only save you hours of time, but they do not get tired, skip pages, or take breaks and forget where they left off. In addition, Summation searches through either selected documents or all of your documents, transcripts, and notes simultaneously, and lets you save or print out the results.

Quick Search

The Quick Search line on the home page screen allows you to enter a single word or a combination of words using connectors such as **&** (and) or **/** (or). Simply enter the word and click on the **Search** button to the left to search the active window. If you have selected several elements in the Case Explorer, you can search against all of these at one time. If a transcript is open or the Core Database is your current window, Quick Search will allow you to search through them from the toolbar.

Fuzzy Search

To conduct a Fuzzy Search, enter the word you wish to search for in the **Quick Search** box and then do the following (see Figure 12):

1. Click on the **Fuzzy Search** box. A list of approximate matches appears in a pop-up window.
2. Click on each of the terms in the list that should be included in your search.
3. Click on **Search Transcripts**.[1]

Vocabulary

The **Vocabulary** icon brings up a complete list, in alphabetical order, of all words appearing in transcripts, the database, and ocrBase (see Figure 13). The number of occurrences appears to the right of each word. Click on the word for a list showing each occurrence. Clicking on any one entry brings you to the "hit."

Blended Search

A blended search combines both notes and database summaries into a single search that can be sorted by date, by issue, or by any other selected field in the database form. (Full-text documents such as transcripts and ocrBase are not included in a blended search because they contain no fielded data.) You

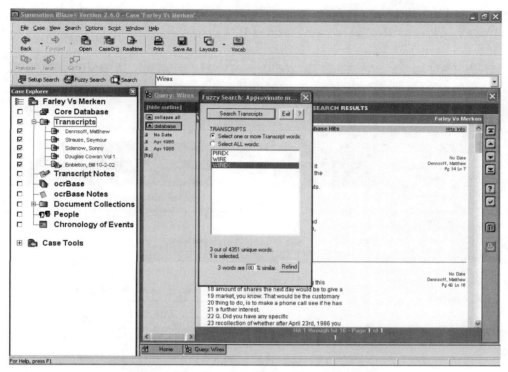

Figure 12. Conducting a Fuzzy Search.

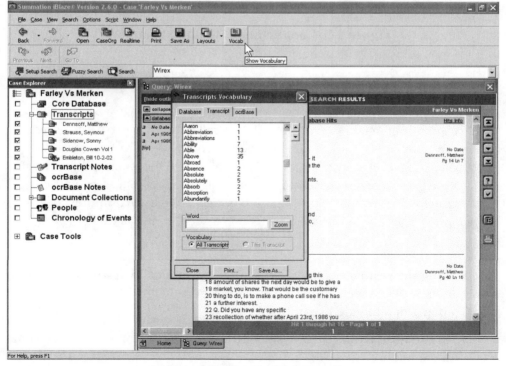

Figure 13. Vocabulary Results.

may also limit the notes and document summaries that are searched only to those marked as HotFacts (see Figure 14).

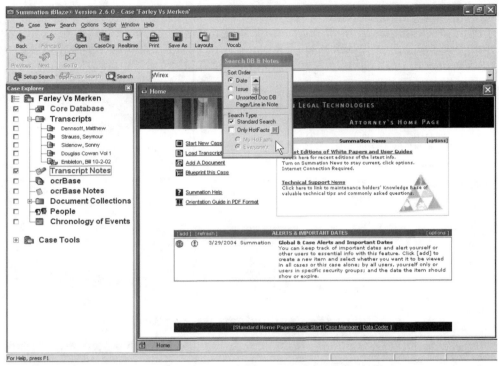

Figure 14. Conducting a Blended Search.

Practice Pointer

Blended searches are considered by many users to be the real strength of Summation. As documents are collected, they can be reviewed by any number of different staff members, all of whom can add notes, comments, or mark items as HotFacts. Later, all of the notes and summaries can then be searched and filtered for specific issues. This can be particularly helpful when looking for specific issues or items that are retrieved and then searched again to see which have been tagged as HotFacts.

Sorting the results of a blended search by date or by issue can result in a unique view of the facts in your case (see Figure 15).

To perform a blended search:

1. In the Case Explorer tree, select the **Transcript Notes** and **Core Database** folders.
2. Enter the search phrase in the **Quick Search** box.

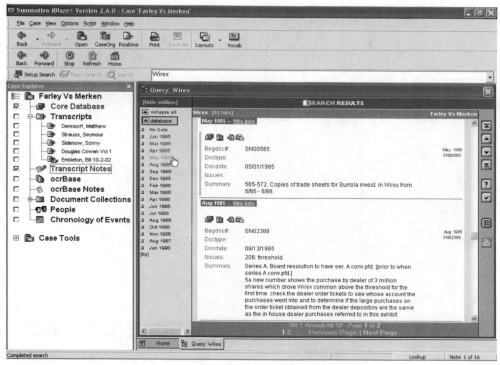

Figure 15. Blended Search Results.

3. When the **Search DB & Notes** dialog appears, select the field by which you want to sort (**Date** or **Issue**).
4. In the **Search Type** section, select what you want to search: all records, all HotFacts, or your own HotFacts.
5. Click on the **Search** button.

Transcripts

Single Transcript

To search a single transcript, double-click on the **Transcripts** folder to obtain a complete list of all transcripts in your case. Click the check-off box at the left (in the Case Explorer panel) to select the transcript to search, and then proceed by entering your search query in the search box above the transcript (see Figure 16).

Multiple Transcripts

To search multiple transcripts, repeat the procedure for single transcripts but click the check-off box to the left of each transcript (in the Case Explorer panel) you wish to search. To search all transcripts, click the check box to the left of the **Transcripts** folder (see Figure 17).

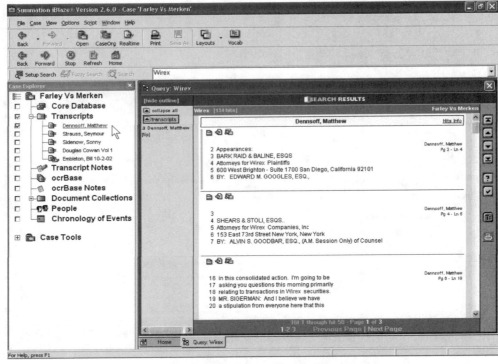

Figure 16. Searching a Single Transcript.

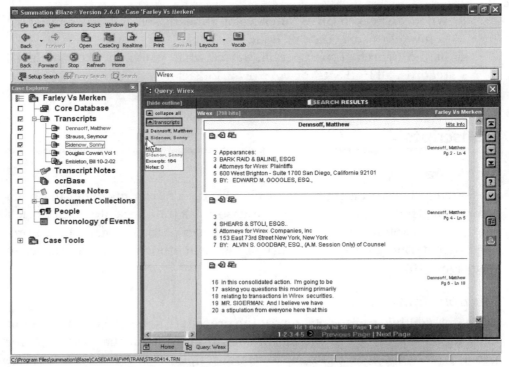

Figure 17. Searching Multiple Transcripts.

Saving a Search

If you have a search you wish to run on an ongoing basis, you can save the search query for future access. After you have run a search, simply right-click on the **Searches** icon in the Case Tools section of the Case Explorer tree. Select **Save Integrated Search,** assign a name and description to the search, and specify whether to save it with the currently checked folders. Once saved, the query is placed under the **Searches** icon and will run when you click on its icon.

Searching Notes

A Quick Search of notes can be performed by checking the box next to **Transcript Notes** in the Case Explorer tree. For more complex searches, click the **Search** menu and select **Notes,** then **Find Note** to bring up the **Find Note** dialog.

Each of the fields in a note database record is included in the **Find Note** dialog (see Figure 18). You can choose whether to view the notes in the note

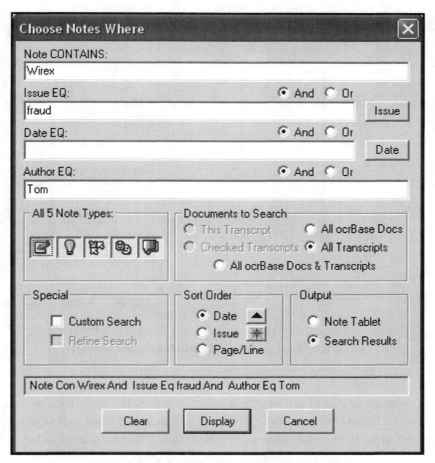

Figure 18. Find Notes Dialog Box.

tablet format (the format used when you create a note), or in the same format as a Quick Search report. The **Find Note** dialog also gives you options for sorting the notes that you retrieve.

Searching the Database

The database has three search options: the standard Quick Search query and two other Core Database Queries available under the **Search → Document Database** menu. The first is a Click and Find query builder that allows you to select entries from pop-up look-up tables in order to build a complex search (see Figures 19 to 21).

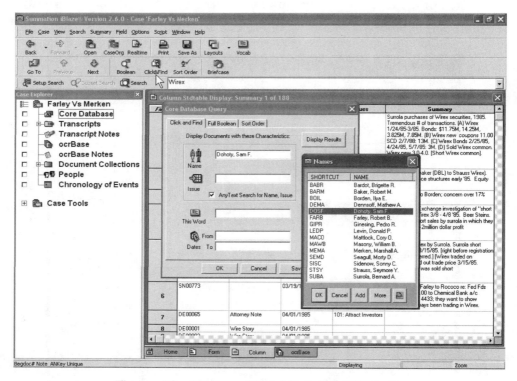

Figure 19. Click and Find Database Search.

The second database search option is a Full Boolean search, which allows you to build the same type of query as Click and Find, but you select the fields and type in the information yourself (see Figures 22 and 23).

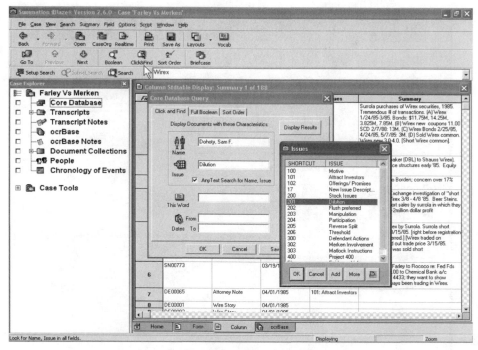

Figure 20. Click and Find Database Search.

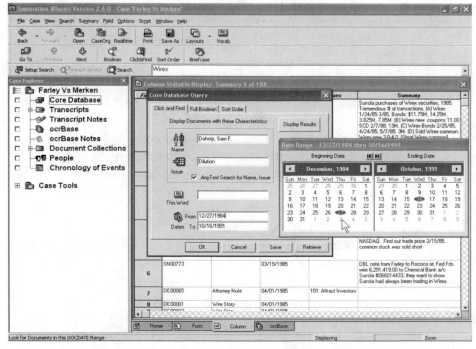

Figure 21. Click and Find Database Search.

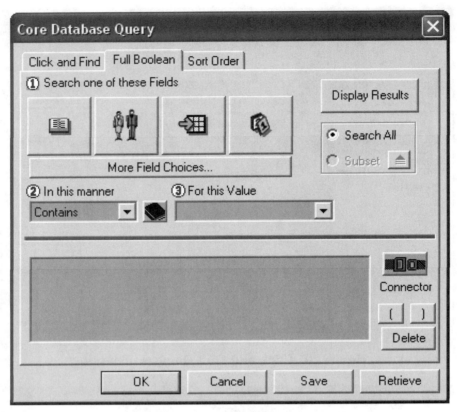

Figure 22. Full Boolean Database Search.

Practice Pointer

One of the most difficult tasks a lawyer faces during litigation is responding to a question that addresses a new fact or an issue that the lawyer did not include in his or her own trial notebook. In the foreword to this book, lawyer Jon Sigerman mentions a trial where the judge asked both sides a question they did not anticipate. His opposing counsel, relying on a traditional trial notebook prepared according to his view of the case, was unable to answer. Mr. Sigerman was able to use Summation to retrieve an exhibit supporting his position.

Why was he able to do this? Because Summation allows you to search all the information, not just the portion you used to prepare for trial. The Column View (or grid) search is not locked into the subset of the evidence that was prepared for trial. After retrieving all documents in a grid view, you can reorder the list by simply clicking on a column heading. You can then obtain a list of all documents ordered by date, document number, or issue, and quickly respond to any unanticipated question.

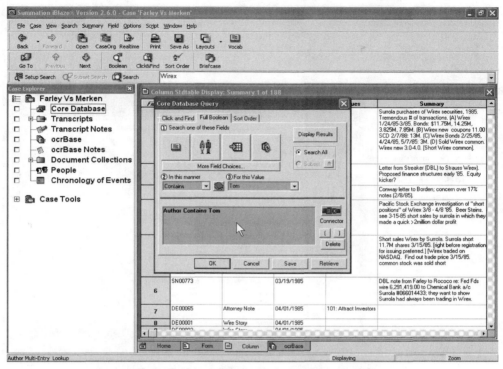

Figure 23. Full Boolean Database Search.

Central Case Directory

You can easily search an entire case or just the core case. The distinction between the two is that the *entire case* includes all the folders in the Case Explorer tree, while the *core case* includes transcripts, transcript notes, the Core Database, the ocrBase, all notes, eDocs, and eMail (see Figure 24). (The core case does *not* include any document collections such as Companion or Remote databases or Briefcased records. A discussion of these can be found in Appendix B.)

To perform a search of the entire case:

1. Enter the search phrase in the **Quick Search** box.
2. Select all the folders in your case by right-clicking on the case name at the top of the Case Explorer tree and clicking on **Check All.**

To perform a search of the core case:

1. Enter the search phrase in the **Quick Search** box.
2. Open the **Search** menu and select **Core Case.**[2]

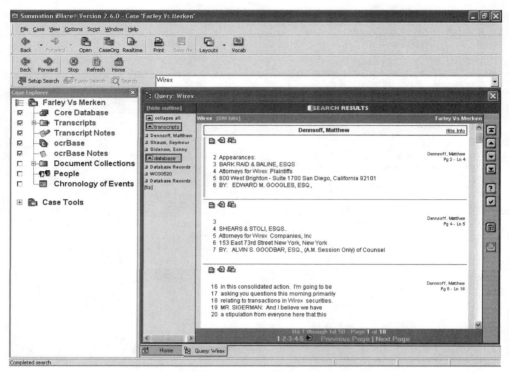

Figure 24. Core Case Search Results.

Notes

1. Summation runs the Fuzzy Search containing each of the terms you selected. If the list does not reflect the words you expected (too few or too many), you may change the "fuzzy percentage" by entering a new number in the percentage text box at the bottom of the dialog.

2. Keep this in mind when conducting searches: the view that is currently active dictates how the results of your search are presented. If the Case Explorer is active, then the search results will appear in the Search Results View. If the Column View is active, then you will see the search results in the grid (or columnar) format. If the Form View is active, the search results will be compiled, but you will only see the first document summary in the Form View.

Part

II

Popular Features

Transcripts 5

Realtime

A Realtime transcript session occurs when a court reporter connects his or her stenograph machine directly to a lawyer's laptop computer so that the ongoing transcription appears live on the connected laptop while it is being typed. Summation's Realtime view has a look and feel similar to Summation's transcript view, with page formatting, notes, and the current line of testimony all clearly indicated.

The Realtime toolbar provides tools specifically applicable to Realtime sessions. The list of tools can be viewed by right-clicking on the white **Quick Search** bar (see Figure 25).

In addition, while the Realtime session is running, you may mark lines of testimony in one of three ways:

- ◆ **Quick Mark.** Pressing the keyboard spacebar creates an empty note on the active line of testimony. You can return later and add comments to the note.
- ◆ **AutoMark.** Specific words or phrases can be preset to automatically mark with color codes during the Realtime session.[1]
- ◆ **Issue-coded Note.** You can add issue-coded notes to the Realtime transcript by using an Issues List (see Figure 26), which assigns either colored buttons or numbers to use for adding the notes.

A Realtime transcript search is done the same as any other Summation transcript search, and you may search during a live Realtime session.[2]

Practice Pointer

In the traditional manner of practice, a lawyer takes notes during a deposition, waits for a hard copy of the transcript to arrive, then retrieves the notes as a reference while reading and marking up a copy of the transcript. A deposition summary may then be prepared through dictation by the lawyer or review by a paralegal, with the notes added in or appended to the summary. This process may occur weeks or even months after the actual deposition, during which time memory fades and notes may be lost.

The Summation Realtime feature offers lawyers an unprecedented ability to capture their thoughts and impressions of testimony and then link them directly to the transcript while the deposition is underway. They can then access both the transcript and the notes immediately after the deposition ends.

There is no better way to handle deposition testimony than this method of identifying issues and recording your thoughts "live" during the event. As lawyer Bil Kellermann, the professional development manager at Summation, said when discussing this point, "You never know more than when you are in the room."

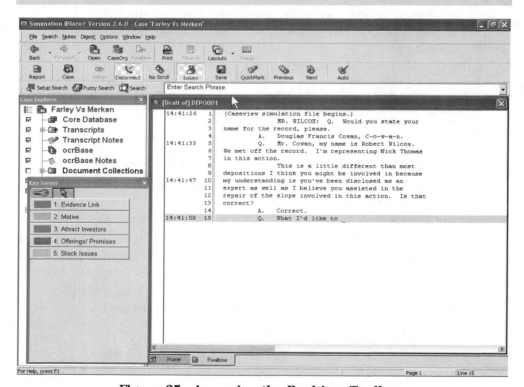

Figure 25. Accessing the Realtime Toolbar.

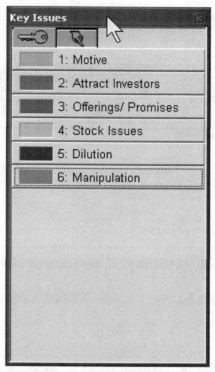

Figure 26. Key Issues List.

Right-Mouse Button Functions

Three popular right-mouse button functions have already been discussed:

- **Copy to Clipboard** (see "Digest Files" in Chapter 3)
- **Write to Digest** (see "Digest Files" in Chapter 3)
- **Copy Excerpt into New Note** (see "Rapid-Fire Digesting" in Chapter 3)

Other right-mouse button functions include the following:

- **Copy Excerpt to Outline.** You can send a transcript excerpt to the Case Organizer at any time. Before beginning your transcript search, open the Case Organizer in the lower Case Explorer window and select the tab for the view you want to use. Leave the Case Organizer window open, and open the transcript. When you want to send a block of testimony from the Realtime transcript to the Case Organizer outline, highlight it and right-click. From the context menu that appears, select **Copy Excerpt to Outline** and the text is copied to the end of the case outline (see Figures 27 and 28). The excerpt can then be dragged and dropped to the appropriate hierarchy in the outline. A link is automatically created from the excerpt back to the transcript.

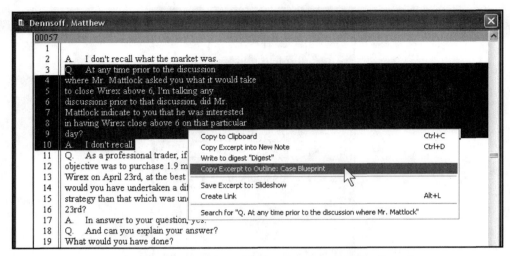

Figure 27. Selecting "Copy Excerpt to Outline."

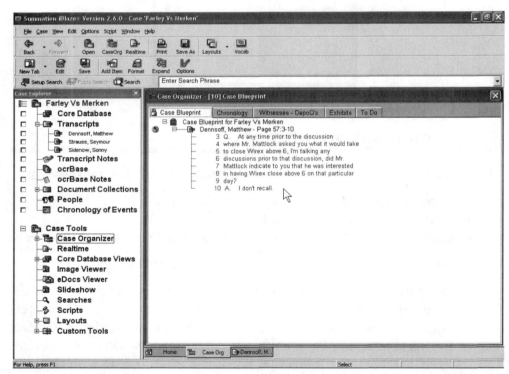

Figure 28. Text Copied to Case Outline Using "Copy Excerpt to Outline."

◆ **Save Excerpt to Slideshow.** The Slideshow Folder feature offers several options for accessing images that are used on a recurring basis. For example, you can create folders based on a specific issue, a witness, a hearing, or a deposition, with images used for these points located in the folder.

To create a new Slideshow folder, right-click on **Slideshow** under Case Tools in the Case Explorer, select **Create New,** and choose **Folder.** Choose **Slideshow** from the drop-down list of folder types and rename the folder by entering a new name in the **Folder Name** text box. Because the images in the Slideshow folder can be rearranged using drag-and-drop, this is an ideal location for organizing images you wish to present using a large monitor or projector. You can arrange the images in the order you wish to display them, show the images in full-screen mode, and navigate forward and backward through the images in the Selected Images folder with a keystroke.[3]

You may copy an excerpt of testimony from a transcript and save it to a slideshow. In this manner, the testimony and the image can appear sequentially in your presentation.

To add a transcript excerpt to the slideshow, simply highlight the excerpt, right-click it, and select **Save Excerpt to Slideshow**. Then enter a description (see Figure 29).

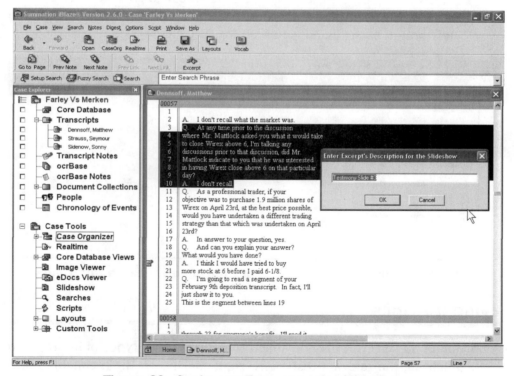

Figure 29. Saving an Excerpt to the Slideshow.

- ◆ **Create Link**. Links are discussed in detail below in the section "Evidence Links."
- ◆ **Search For.** Right-clicking on any word or phrase automatically brings up a dialog box prompting you to search for that word or phrase (see Figure 30).

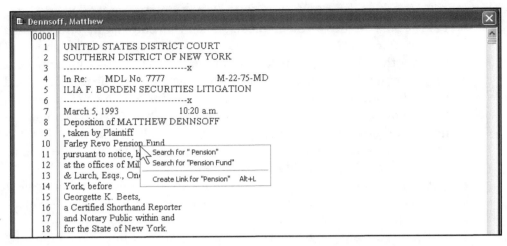

Figure 30. Right-clicking to bring up "Search for" dialog.

◆ Likewise, left-clicking and dragging the mouse to create an excerpt and then right-clicking on that excerpt brings up the right-click menu. The last option in the menu is **Search for** (see Figure 31).

Figure 31. Right-clicking on Excerpt to bring up "Search for" dialog.

Evidence Links

A portion of a transcript may be linked to various other types of information by highlighting the relevant testimony, right-clicking on the highlighted segment, and selecting **Create Link**, which brings up the **Link to** dialog (see Figure 32).

You may then select the target for the linked testimony, which can be

◆ A line in another transcript (a cue card opens with instructions)
◆ A video clip of a transcript (the Windows **Open File** dialog box opens; navigate to the specific mpg file and click on it to create the link)

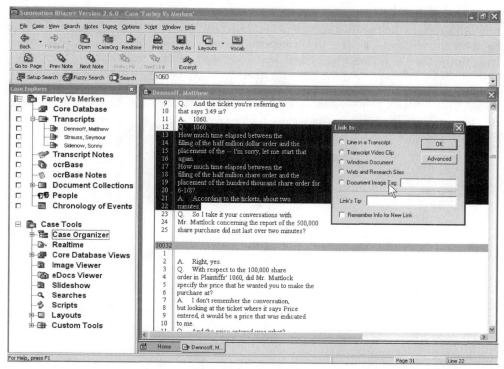

Figure 32. Create a Link.

♦ A Windows document (the Windows **Open File** dialog box opens; navigate to the specific document file and click on it to create the link)

♦ A Web site (enter the URL of the site)

♦ An image (the database Column View opens and a cue card appears with instructions)

Once a link target is selected, Summation fills in the **Link's Tip** text box based on the selected target; you may modify this text. That text will then appear as a tip when you position your cursor over the testimony that has been linked. (If you wish to use the same target for several links, select **Remember Info for New Link.** When you create the next link, the target information and Link's Tip will be filled in for you, based on the target you used first.)

Links can also be created by a court reporter during a Realtime deposition session, or automatically created using a script.

Notes

1. A patent claim that indirectly involves the concept of automarking but does *not* involve Summation has been made against several court-reporting companies. Based on the advice of counsel, Summation management believes that neither Summation's products, nor use of those products by court reporters, lawyers, and other professionals infringes upon any valid patent claim. For more information, contact Summation at 800-735-7866.

2. Summation also provides a simulated Realtime file that allows you to practice using this feature. It is available by double-clicking the **Realtime** button in the lower Case Explorer window and following the prompts to create a session. In the **Setup Options** dialog, select **I want to try a demo of Realtime using a simulated transcription**.

3. Note, however, that the items in a slideshow folder are *not* the original images. They are, instead, pointers to the original images wherever they are stored. Thus if you put watermarks or Bates numbers on an image you call up through a link to the database and that image has been placed in a slideshow folder, the changes will appear in the slideshow "version" as well.

OCRBase

6

Optical Character Recognition (OCR) is the process that uses software to convert scanned electronic pictures (or images) of documents into searchable text documents. If a standard paper copy of a typical business letter is scanned, the image of the letter can be linked to a database record in Summation, but the contents of the letter cannot be directly searched because it is only an image. To perform word searches on the letter, it must be run through OCR software that uses character recognition methods (matching the patterns of the shapes in the picture with stored sets of characters) to translate the image of the letter into computer text. That text can then be searched.[1]

So in order to use Summation's ocrBase, your documents first must be imaged and then run through OCR software. This can be done within your firm, by a service bureau, or on the fly with images that are already linked to a Summation database. The full-text documents are then loaded into Summation and indexed using the Blaze function, Summation's proprietary indexing tool.

Once this process is complete, you can search for words or phrases within the documents. You may also attach notes to documents, just as you do with transcripts. Also, using Summation's image viewer in conjunction with ocrBase, you can view documents in their original form (the image) *and* conduct full-text searches (the OCR'd version). This combination helps to reduce labor-intensive document coding.

Note

1. Because OCR'd documents commonly contain misinterpreted characters due to the poor quality of the original document (for example, an *H* is blurry and mistaken for a *4*, or a coffee stain partially obscures an *e* making it look like a *c*), the use of the Fuzzy Search is well-suited for OCR'd documents since they afford the opportunity to search for near-matches to your search term(s).

Electronic Evidence

7

Because so many documents in today's electronic workplace are created electronically, many discovery requests result in the production of what Summation calls eDocs. Simply put, these are evidentiary documents in an electronic rather than a paper format. They may include Microsoft Word documents, database records, or e-mail messages, all in their original electronic format.

Summation can process and load these eDocs automatically. The processing step (using Summation's eDiscovery Console)[1] allows Summation to find the electronic documents when you are ready to produce them electronically. It also gives you the opportunity to use a central location to manage the first step in processing and loading eDiscovery, and provides the audit trail for authenticity purposes.

Once loaded, a document database record is created for each document. The eDocs can be viewed either as plain text or in their original format using the program in which they were created, as long as that program is installed on your system. All eDocs are searchable from the Case Explorer and are automatically Blazed each time you load them (see Figure 33).

You can search eDocs and eMail from the Case Explorer by checking any combination of eMail, eDocs, and eMail attachments. Enter your search phrase in the **Quick Search** box and click on **Search**. Search results are displayed with a specific icon indicating that the result is an eDoc.

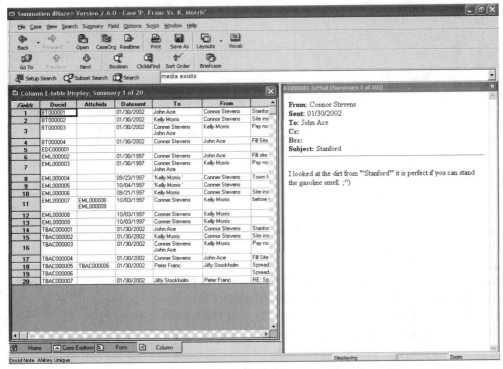

Figure 33. Viewing e-Docs.

Practice Pointer

Electronic discovery presents an entirely new method of handling discovery documents. One of the greatest challenges it presents is the concept of document numbering. Unlike paper documents, which are traditionally numbered on each individual page, an electronic document captured, for example, from an e-mail file, does not have "pages" until it is printed out.

Summation looks at these documents from the perspective of unitization or document breaks. The relevant numbers in the database then become the DocID and document range numbers, and not the traditional Bates number on each page.

Note

1. The eDiscovery Console is discussed in greater detail in the Appendix A.

Orchestrating Your Case

8

Once the various data components of a case have been assembled, Summation offers a powerful way to work with that data. The quick and easy access to all case information provides a method of profiling a case that is unique to Summation.

In addition to the ability to search across all case data simply by checking off items in the Case Explorer, there are several new Case Organizer tools, including the following:

 ◆ **Chronology of Events Table.** A standard tool available in the Case Explorer that is created with every case, the Chronology of Events captures critical information about events and people throughout your case (see Figure 34). It allows immediate adding, editing, sorting, linking, and tracking of case events, including color-coding of events for quick categorization and retrieval. Document database summaries and transcripts can be linked to events in this table for instant reference.

 ◆ **People Table**. This tool is also available in the Case Explorer and is created with every case. The People Table (Figure 35) opens in a grid similar to the database Column View, where each row in the grid is a separate person and each column is a field in the entry. The People Table allows you to work simultaneously with multiple entries, and from this view you may add new entries, edit existing entries, or change the grid itself.

 ◆ **Quick Action Tools**. These tools allow you to zoom directly from a search hit to an actual case component,

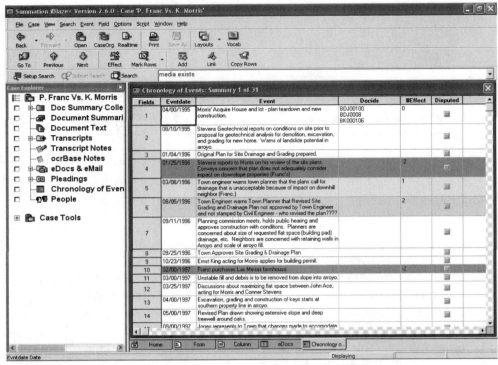

Figure 34. Chronology of Events Table.

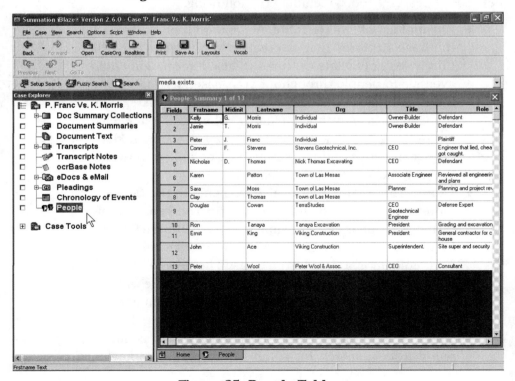

Figure 35. People Table.

such as the database, transcript, or notes (see Figure 36). Depending upon the case component being displayed, you can view an image, zoom into the underlying record, or copy to the Case Organizer. To return to the search results, simply click on the **Query** tab.

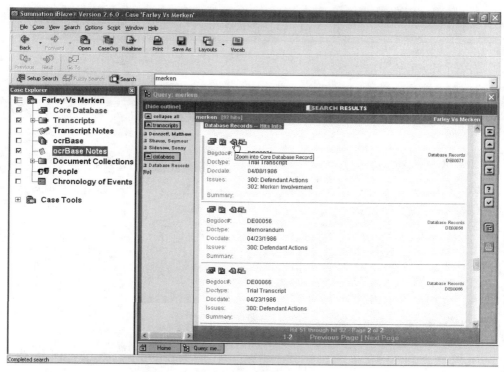

Figure 36. Quick Action Tools.

Part

III

Using Summation

Using Summation in Your Practice

9

Okay, so you've read the chapters on specific Summation functions and you think you understand how the basic program features work. But you still aren't quite sure how to actually sit down and use it. Before you even open the program, it may help to think about how you work.

As a litigator, you process large amounts of information to find the data that supports your case, and then use that data to help prepare a persuasive argument. Summation breaks this process down into three functions: organize, search, and orchestrate.

Organize

You can organize the raw data that continuously arrives as a case progresses, and use Summation to

- ◆ Capture key evidentiary items
- ◆ Annotate data with work-product thoughts
- ◆ Assign issues
- ◆ Organize into outlines
- ◆ Review a transcript and annotate the testimony

Search

Summation provides a single point of access for searching all the information underlying your litigation. Using the Case Explorer, you can

- Search for a word or phrase in a particular transcript
- Search for related issues in both a transcript and a document collection
- Search a remote document or transcript repository over the Internet
- Zoom into any discrete element of evidence or testimony, and retreat back to the report
- Be presented with an integrated report showing "hits" in each of the components

Orchestrate

You can then prepare your case using the above tools to

- Review and excerpt the record of personal narrative in the case by annotating transcripts
- Review and subjectively analyze the physical and documentary evidence in a case and select it for production or presentation
- Create chronologies of critical factual events that convey the story of the case in the most understandable way
- Create outlines for briefs, arguments, witness preparation, examinations, and the like, to marshal your thoughts into cohesive and intelligent work product

Summation does all this by using a ***case metaphor***. The Case Explorer window (see Figure 37) contains the folders of information for the case you are working on. You can very easily shift to another case by right-clicking on the **Case Folder File Cabinet** icon (just below the Case Explorer heading).

The various types of information associated with a case—including transcripts, discovery document summaries, electronic documents as image files, text files (from OCR or otherwise), electronic evidence such as e-mail, and abstracts describing physical evidence—are assigned to dedicated folders. Subcomponents of a folder (including transcripts, document collections from local repositories, document collections from remote repositories, and Briefcases created from a local document collection or downloaded over the Internet from a remote repository) can be accessed by expanding the folder.

From this view, you can begin by opening a new case, then load transcripts and documents as discussed in Chapter 1. You then proceed by using

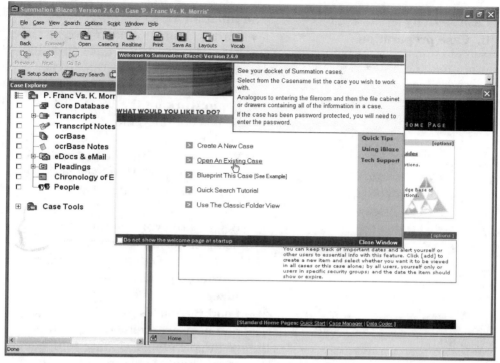

Figure 37. The Case Explorer Window.

the Case Explorer as a litigation "command center" to display and organize all items in a case, and as a starting point for searches.

Case Timeline

The Case Timeline shown in the Summation **Help** menu displays a chronology of events a litigator might encounter when working on a typical case. Let's walk through this timeline to show you the various Summation processes that you may wish to use at each stage of the litigation. Each case is different, and each user has his or her own way of working, so think of this as a guideline to using the many features of Summation.

Starting the Case

Case Activity	Summation Tasks
I. Intake of case (filing of Complaint, answer)	◆ **Start a new Summation case** ◆ Set up **case-level security**, if appropriate (*for **network** administrators on a concurrent user version*)

Case Activity	Summation Tasks
II. Case preparation	◆ Start adding information to the **Case Blueprint** tab in the **Case Organizer** ◆ Start adding tasks to the "To Do" tab in **Case Organizer** ◆ **Begin work on the Issues list** (to be incorporated into the Issues Lookup **table** ◆ Begin work on the **cast of characters** in the **Core Database** and **list of key names** for the Names Lookup Table ◆ Begin early work on the chronology using either the **Chronology form in the Core Database** or using the **Chronology tab in the Case Organizer** ◆ **Load the case's pleadings** for quick and easy searching of the content of the pleadings. Update as needed throughout the course of the litigation. ◆ Set up **Internet Resources Links** to your local court rules (if on the Internet), to opposing and co-counsel's web sites, and to other Internet sites that may be useful to you throughout the case ◆ Identify other related case databases *in* the office for possible access as **Companion Databases*** and other pertinent databases that may exist *outside* the office for possible access as **Remote Databases.*** *Access to Companion Databases is available to users of Summation **Blaze** LG Gold and Summation iBlaze editions. Access to Remote Databases is available to users of Summation iBlaze.
III. Coordination with co-counsel	◆ Discussions among attorneys and Information Technology staff about sharing of data (possible use of a repository such as **CaseVault** or **Remote Databases***) *Access to remote repositories and databases is available to users of the Summation iBlaze edition.

Investigation

Case Activity	Summation Tasks
I. Interviews of client and employees	◆ Begin insertion of names into **Names Lookup Table** ◆ Consider **converting word-processed interview memoranda** into Summation for easy searching and cross-referencing ◆ Create a **transcript group** in the **Case Explorer** to hold unsworn witness interviews (converted word processing documents) ◆ Build the **Issues Lookup Table** ◆ **Set up layouts** that you may wish to use during this phase of the case and **save them to the Layouts folder**. ◆ Use **Issues Lookup Table** to **issue-code key witness interview memoranda** that were converted into Summation ◆ Create **Evidence Links** in the converted interview memoranda to tie together related pieces of your client's story based on interviews
II. Review of client documents	◆ Review **Core Database standard form** to determine whether customization is required or desirable. If so, **modify the standard form or add additional forms**, as your case requires. ◆ **Set** up an outline in the **Case Organizer** to reflect information the users may need when working with the **Core Database**, such as purposes of the various fields, anticipated scheduling for data entry, etc. On a **network** system, this area can serve as a great method to keep team members updated on database issues and modifications.

Case Activity	Summation Tasks
II. Review of client documents (*continued*)	◆ Begin **customizing the Doctype Lookup Table** based on your review of the client documents ◆ Begin **building the documents database** by summarizing key client documents in the Core Database ◆ Begin **imaging** your client's documents and **loading them into Summation** ◆ Continue adding to **Cast of Characters form** ◆ Continue adding to **Chronology** form
III. Conduct non-party witness interviews	◆ Consider **converting word-processed interview memoranda** into Summation for easy searching and cross-referencing ◆ Create a **transcript group** in the **Case Explorer** for unsworn witness interviews (if not done so already) ◆ Use **Issues Lookup Table** to **issue-code key witness interview memoranda** that were converted into Summation ◆ Create **Evidence Links** in the converted interview memoranda to tie together related pieces of witness's stories
IV. Obtain non-party documents	◆ Continue adding to **Chronology form** as new information arises in non-party documents. ◆ **Image non-party documents**, as appropriate. ◆ **Add non-party documents to database**, as appropriate. ◆ Add substantive affidavits to the **Core Database**, as **full-text documents in the Transcripts folder**, or OCR* them for full-text searching *Summation's **ocrBase** is available in the Summation **Blaze** LG Gold and iBlaze editions.

Case Activity	Summation Tasks
V. **Search for experts**	◆ Access the firm's Expert Witness Databank. (Your firm may maintain an Expert Witness Databank as a "case" in Summation, in an Access **database**, or in a SQL Server 7 database. You can include a **Companion Database link*** in your current case to the Expert Witness Databank, if you wish.) ◆ Conduct searches on the Internet. (See the Internet links on the **Home Page** for some web sites to get you started.) *Companion database access is available to users of Summation Blaze LG Gold and Summation iBlaze editions.

The Discovery Phase

Case Activity	Summation Tasks
I. **Document Productions and Document Management**	◆ **Search the database** to identify client documents to be produced ◆ **OCR** interrogatory responses and responses to requests for production of documents for easy searching using **ocrBase*** ◆ **Build on the Lookup Tables**: Names, DocType, Properties, and others ◆ Continue adding to the **Cast of Characters and Chronology** ◆ Add at least two tabs to the **Case Organizer**: one to track document production information (dates, document number ranges, etc.) and one to track deposition information: who, when, where and then follow-up on disks, video, transcripts ◆ **Summarize the basic (objective) information** about the documents coming in through document productions

Case Activity	Summation Tasks
I. Document Productions and Document Management (*continued*)	◆ Create production sets of documents and images, renumbering the documents as needed using the **Production Numbering Tool**
	◆ **Add subjective information to the summaries** of key documents (issues, priority, attorney comments). **Save a layout** using the **Review Form** and the **Image View** in tandem.
	◆ **HotFact important documents**, which can be used as you prepare for depositions or trial exhibits lists.
	◆ Identify privileged, work product and other protected documents, including those covered by confidentiality agreements and protective orders. Add the information to the Privilege **field** in the **Core Database's standard form** or create a new, separate **database** of privileged documents which can then be used as a **Companion Database.****
	◆ Keep track of documents covered by protective orders for end-of-case handling by entering "Confidential" (or similar terminology) in the Privilege field of the **Core Database's standard form**.
	◆ Load **electronic documents** and **e-mail files** produced by other parties
	◆ Continue **imaging** (and **OCRing**, if appropriate) incoming documents produced through supplemental discovery.

Case Activity	Summation Tasks
I. Document Productions and Document Management (*continued*)	◆ Prepare a **privilege log** using the **Privilege field to locate privileged documents** or a separate privileged documents database *ocrBase is available to users of the Summation **Blaze** LG Gold and iBlaze versions **Access to Companion Databases is available to users of Summation Blaze LG Gold and Summation iBlaze editions.
II. Depositions	◆ **Identify documents** to be used in upcoming depositions. **Briefcase* the documents by witness** and **batch print images,** if appropriate. ◆ **Save frequently accessed and key images** in the Slideshow folder in the Case Explorer. ◆ Access remote or repository databases** to search for potential exhibits. Briefcase** records and images as needed. ◆ Prepare witness outlines in the **Case Organizer, including** excerpts from transcripts, the document database. ◆ Use **RealTime** at the depositions. Get a jump on issue-coding using the **AutoMark** function. ◆ **Load (or update draft) deposition transcripts** as they come in ◆ **Issue-code depositions** as they come in ◆ Link important deposition exhibits to key deposition testimony ◆ **Create Image Links** back to deposition testimony relating to the imaged exhibits ◆ Use **excerpts** and the **issues lists** to begin creation of witness "books" ◆ Review the issues covered in the depositions to date by producing **Issues List reports** or **issues-based Digests**

Case Activity	Summation Tasks
II. Depositions (*continued*)	◆ Continue adding to the **Chronology** database or the **Chronology tab (Case Organizer)** based on deposition testimony ◆ Continue adding knowledge gleaned from deposition testimony to the **Cast of Characters** ◆ Use Notes to handle **deposition errata** submitted by witnesses ◆ Enter **deposition exhibit numbers and witness information in the Core Database** for documents used as exhibits ◆ Continue building on the **Case Blueprint in the Case Organizer** ◆ Run **"blended searches"** of the documents and notes (including **transcript excerpts**), based on key terms, issues, names. **Save often used search queries**. ◆ Begin identifying key documents to be included in the Trial Exhibits List. **Edit** Doctitles, as needed, for creation of the Trial Exhibits List. *Access to Briefcasing is available to users of Summation iBlaze. **Access to remote and repository databases and to Briefcasing is available to users of Summation iBlaze.
III. Discovery Hearings	◆ Use information in the **database** and the **Case Organizer** to prepare and respond to discovery motions

Pre-Trial: Motions Practice and Heraings

Case Activity	Summation Tasks
I. Dispositive motions, motions in limine and hearings	◆ **Conduct integrated** searches of documents, **transcript notes**, and testimony to strategize

Case Activity	Summation Tasks
I. Dispositive motions, motions in limine and hearings (*continued*)	◆ Conduct searches on key facts, using the **blended sort feature** to **limit** the result to only HotFacts and to sort the results in order to capture the facts that best support your motion or controvert theirs ◆ Create a tab in **Case Organizer** to hold your outline for the brief, including pertinent transcript and document references ◆ **Conduct multi-transcript searches to locate testimony** and use **transcript excerpts** to support the argument(s); use the **Issues field** to flag the testimony; copy excerpts into the appropriate **Case Organizer** outline ◆ Use the **Issues field** to flag documents that may be used as exhibits to the briefs ◆ **Print images of documents** to be used as exhibits to the brief and for hearing notebook ◆ Use the **Transcript Cites** feature to print transcript pages with underlined text references to be used as exhibits to the brief and for hearing notebook

Pre-Trial: Witness and Exhibits Lists

Case Activity	Summation Tasks
II. Prepare exhibits lists	◆ **Continue identifying documents** to be used as trial exhibits and editing the Doctitle field page as needed ◆ Depending upon volume, **print images of exhibits** (or send to a vendor for printing) ◆ **Print the exhibits list** (using the Doctitle field, among others) for distribution to counsel and the court

Case Activity	Summation Tasks
II. Prepare exhibits lists (*continued*)	◆ **Create a Trial Exhibits form** based on the standard **form** keep track of disposition of exhibits during trial (status, court's rulings, and so on)
III. Prepare witness list	◆ Use the **Cast of Characters** and **witness-coded transcript notes** to identify witnesses

Settlement

Case Activity	Summation Tasks
I. Prepare settlement offer or response	◆ Create a Settlement outline in **Case Organizer** ◆ **Search the Core and Remote Databases, transcripts, and transcript notes** for key facts to support or respond to a settlement offer. **Copy, as needed, to the Settlement outline in Case Organizer.** ◆ **Save key images into the Slideshow folder and arrange as needed for presentation at Settlement Conference**
II. Settlement Conference	◆ Use **Settlement outline** and **Selected Images folder** to present your position at the settlement conference

Trial

Case Activity	Summation Tasks
I. Exhibits preparation, presentation and tracking	◆ **Locate** and, if imaged, **print** for the Court's **record** documents being used as exhibits ◆ Add the next day's exhibit images to the **Selected Images folder** for presentation ◆ Use **Markup Tools** to highlight key points in imaged exhibits

Case Activity	Summation Tasks
I. Exhibits preparation, presentation and tracking (*continued*)	◆ Use **saved formats** to retrieve on a witness-by-witness basis the list of exhibits being used with each witness. Track status of exhibits each day in court using the Trial Exhibits form
II. Examination of witnesses	◆ Use **Case Organizer** to fine-tune examination and cross-examination outlines ◆ **Search witness transcripts** for impeachment testimony. Use the **Translide** feature to save the excerpts to individual witness Slideshow folders. ◆ Connect to the court reporter's system with **Realtime** for immediate access to **live feed** of witness testimony. Use Quick Marks, Automarks, and **key Issues** list to prepare for impeachment and follow-up questions. ◆ **Update Realtime drafts** with finalized transcripts of the proceedings

Post-Trial

Case Activity	Summation Tasks
Return of confidential documents	◆ Print a list of the confidential documents produced to and by you in the course of the case. This provides you with a checklist to retrieve confidential documents from opposing counsel or to return confidential documents that you may have received.
Appeal (if any)	◆ Confirm official transcripts of proceedings are **loaded** into Summation ◆ Outline argument in **Case Organizer**, inserting ____ from the official **record** to support your position

Case Activity	Summation Tasks
Case Closure	◆ Save Summation case folder for archival purposes onto storage media ◆ **Remove the case** from Summation's case listing

Native-File Electronic Document Discovery

E-mail messages make up the majority of day-to-day electronic document discovery (EDD). E-mail messages are often acquired in e-mail stores (such as a Microsoft Outlook PST file). Native e-mail stores are not conducive to management and analysis in a litigation support system. E-mail messages must be processed to effectively manage, search, review, and produce them. The processing employed is delivered in one of three ways:

- ◆ Class 1—Paper Paradigm: The e-mail store is deconstructed, converted into an image file format and searchable full-text is extracted. The e-mail can then be used in traditional litigation support systems in a fashion similar to scanned paper and OCR text. This represents a traditional though more costly approach, especially if a labor intensive "manual print, scan, and OCR" system is used.
- ◆ Class 2—Native File Paradigm: Forensic consultants or law firm staff deconstruct the e-mail store into electronic components. Extracted data and meta-data are loaded into databases while linked native-file attachments are copied, indexed, and viewed using generic file viewers. The least costly alternative initially, this approach may require further processing of subsets of the document collection to convert them for redaction or presentation purposes.
- ◆ Class 3—Combination Paradigm: The e-mail store is deconstructed into converted image, extracted text, and

electronic formats. While more costly on a per-item basis, this provides the quickest, most flexible approach.

This section uses a simple e-mail store as an example of EDD that needs to be processed. The store includes two e-mail messages. The first message has a Microsoft Excel spreadsheet attached to it, and the second message has two Microsoft Word documents attached to it.

The Client Source Computer System

On the client's authenticating volume, the EDD appears as a Microsoft Outlook Mailbox (PST) file, which contains the e-mail messages and attachments.

PST1.pst

Figure 1. The PST file icon.

In one sense, this single file represents a potentially discoverable document, albeit a large or compound document. It is also thus a collection of smaller documents—the e-mails and attachments making up the store.

Deconstructing the PST

Figure 2 below shows the way a PST mailbox (and the e-mail messages in it) looks when it is broken down into its constituent parts.

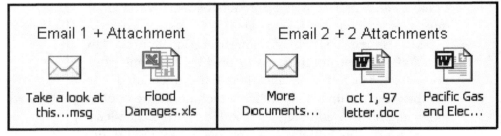

Figure 2. Components cracked from PST1.pst.

Note: At this level, the documents could be assigned Bates numbers for management and control purposes as WGB0001 through WGB0005. Since it is unknown what, if any, page count is represented in any of these documents, they are numbered sequentially as single objects.

Using the eDiscovery Console in Summation

Native file information can be processed by the law firm using the eDiscovery Console in Summation. If the firm wants extensive preprocessing or high-speed conversion to a paper paradigm, either as paper printouts, or as an image and full-text conversion, the PST file can be processed by a third-party electronic discovery consultant or document conversion service bureau.

Regardless of how the firm selects to process the e-mail for ultimate capture as case evidence, the eDiscovery console provides a simple and direct means to sample prospective eDiscovery document collections. This targeted analysis provides the litigator with necessary information to make informed decisions when deploying personnel and financial resources to the eDiscovery process in his or her case.

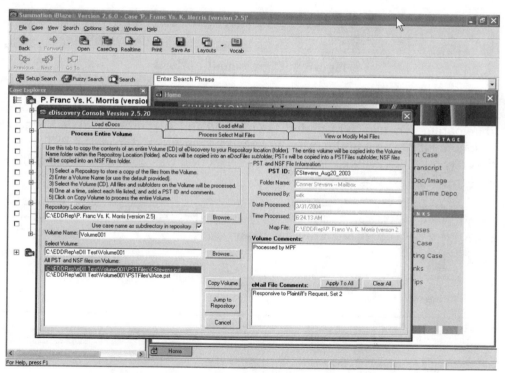

Figure 3. eDiscovery Console processing e-mail.

Information about the PST archive and the steps taken to process the archive are captured at the outset of the process workflow. This allows the firm to track each e-mail or attachment to its source on the authenticating volume provided by the source party.

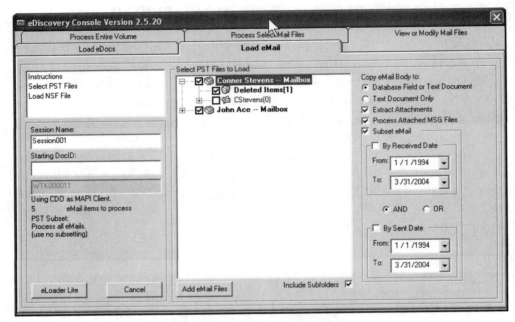

Figure 4. Copy e-mail options.

E-mail and attachments can be processed as entire folder structures or can be loaded sequentially folder by folder. In addition, e-mail outside selected date parameters can be excluded. Each e-mail and attachment will be assigned a document ID value in the order in which it is processed from the PST.

Figure 5 below illustrates that the collection was rendered to image files and that the text was extracted.

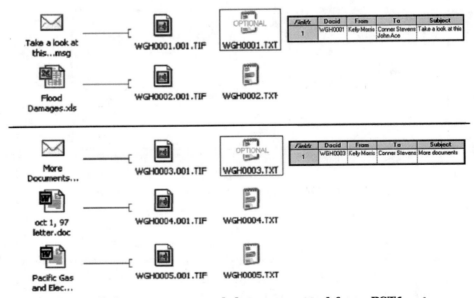

Figure 5. Images, text, and data converted from PST1.pst into document ID values.

In the case of the e-mail message itself, the fielded information that comprises the e-mail message in Microsoft Outlook becomes fielded information housed in the Summation Core Database. The e-mail message is rendered to an image file format, looking the same as it would in printed format. Some systems also extract the text of the e-mail message and save it as an ASCII text file. Appropriate portions or all of this information can be loaded into a Summation case Core Database.

Delivery from the Client Using CD Volumes

While the choices for delivery media abound, most service bureaus presently deliver processed information on CDs. To continue with the example used so far in this document, the information is delivered in a series of three CDs. If the volume of processed information exceeds the space available, you should be provided three *sets* of CDs, broken down as follows:

PST1
Vol001
Vol001_Attachments CD

The following figure illustrates the contents of the first CD or set.

PST1.pst

Figure 6. PST CD.

Figures 7 and 8 on page 72 illustrate the contents of the second and third CDs (or sets), respectively.

Reviewing the E-mail Messages and Attachments in a Summation Case

On receipt of the information from the client or service bureau, litigation staff loads the information using the Summation DII load file. Once loaded, the basic organizational unit is the Summation Core Database record created for each part of the e-mail store generated by service bureau processing. The Core Database can be searched concurrently with the native attachments in

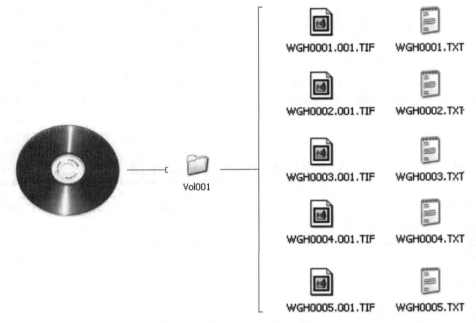

Figure 7. Image files CD.

Note: *If the content of the respective volume exceeds the space available on one CD, multiple CDs can be used.*

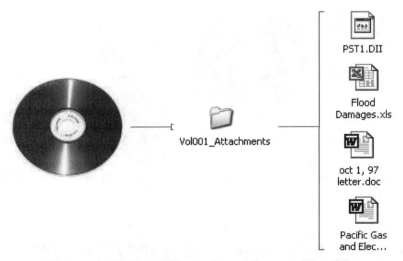

Figure 8. DII load file and attachment files CD.

Note: *While the information represented in the example would easily fit onto one CD in its entirety, dealing with such a limited amount of e-mail messages is unlikely. Since a Microsoft Outlook PST file can hold up to one gigabyte (1 GB) of e-mail data, it is likely that the PST file would fill an entire CD alone. Therefore, a user would need three CDs or more to hold the typical volume of information represented in an e-mail store.*

Summation. Search results can then be expanded to include all family members accompanying a part of an e-mail message (the e-mail message or its attachments) containing the search term. With Summation's Include Family Summaries feature, the parent e-mail message and its child attachments are also displayed even though they may not contain the search term. Furthermore, the parent e-mail message and related attachments are used to create a complete document for either paperless or printed production.

Figure 9 shows the way e-mail information could be displayed once it is properly loaded in the database.

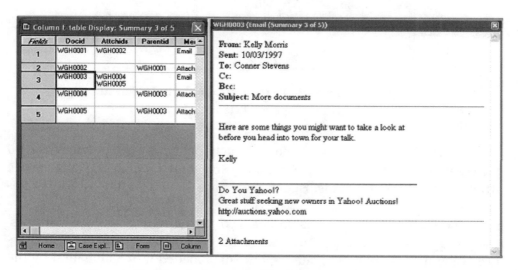

Figure 9. Viewing e-mail and attachment database records in Summation.

Figure 10 shows how an e-mail message looks in Summation.

Figure 10. Viewing an e-mail message in Summation.

Figure 11 shows how an e-mail attachment looks in Summation.

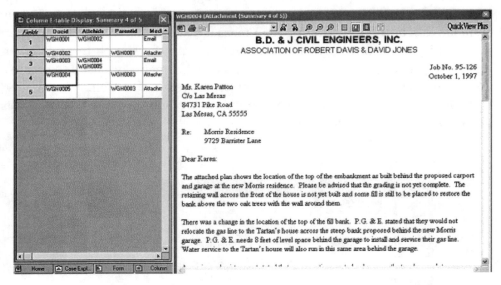

Figure 11. Viewing an e-mail attachment in Summation.

Reviewing Family Summaries in Summation

The following example shows how the relationship between a parent e-mail message and its child attachments is displayed in Summation.

🛏 Column E-table Edit: Summary 1 of 3				
Fields	Docid	Media	Attchids	Parentid
1	WGH0003	Email	WGH0004 WGH0005	
2	WGH0004	Attachment		WGH0003
3	WGH0005	Attachment		WGH0003

Parent Document ⟶

Attachment Documents

Figure 12. Parent-child relationship between an e-mail message and its attachments.

For the Include Family Summaries functionality to work properly, the DII file created for the client must be set up to correctly populate the appropriate **Attchids** and **Parentid** fields. Figure 13 on page 75 further illustrates the parent-child relationship.

The parent-child relationship between the parts of a single e-mail message (the message itself and its attachments) is preserved when the client information processed by the service bureau is loaded into Summation by the DII load file.

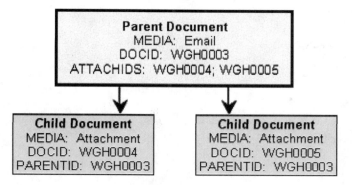

Figure 13. Parent-child relationship.

The processed e-mail native file attachments can be indexed, searched, and displayed in Summation in their native formats along with the e-mail information in the associated record. The advantage of being able to search and view attachments in their native formats is that metadata, hidden messages, and other information are preserved so the reviewer can readily access it.

The following figure shows the docked display of the rendered (imaged) e-mail attachment adjacent to the extracted text window. Redaction tools can be used on the image in the left window. The window on the right shows the rendered, extracted text available from the ocrBase. Annotations can be created in this window. Notice also the page synchronization on the title bars of each window.

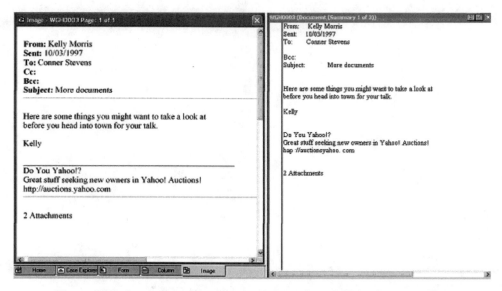

Figure 14. Image and ocrBase views of e-mail in Summation.

Integrated Architecture for Remote Access and Case Collaboration

The main body of this book focuses upon the desktop-license version of Summation software. The desktop version represents the most common way lawyers and paralegals have accessed Summation-hosted information in the past.

Summation has recently completed work on its Integrated Architecture model, which allows lawyers and paralegals to access Summation-hosted case information over the Web. The source of the case information may be either law-firm or third-party hosted, depending upon the needs of the parties and the dynamics of the litigation.

In any case, Summation provides a collection of tools that leverages your time spent learning and your ability to use the software. These tools include

- ◆ LG/iBlaze for the desktop
- ◆ WebBlaze for the law-firm hosted environment
- ◆ CaseVault for the third-party hosted environment

You can learn one software interface for accessing case information. Thereafter you can use the same workflow to perform typical litigation tasks regardless of the means—desktop or browser-based software—made available to you.

The key to the integrated architecture is that the Case Explorer, as well as all of the key elements of a case represented therein, is represented in nearly identical fashion in each Summation software product. Further, products can be mixed and matched to the specific needs of any case without concomitant training and support costs associated with deploying multiple software platforms.

The following discussion exemplifies some of the many similarities between Summation products.

The Case Explorer in WebBlaze

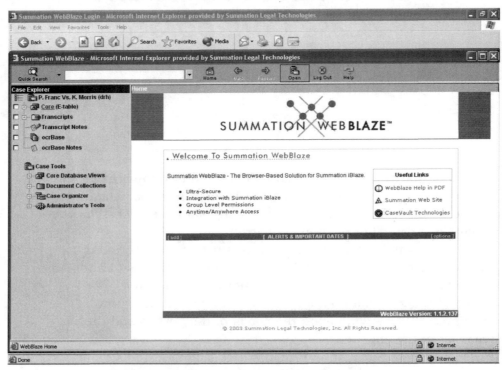

Figure 15. Case Explorer in WebBlaze.

Summation WebBlaze runs exclusively within the Microsoft Internet Explorer browser window. Users require a specific Web page to access, which is hosted by the law firm. Thereafter, users must have a specific login and password to access the case (see Figure 16). Once the lawyer or paralegal authenticates into the secure system, he or she can work in tandem with other users accessing the case from the Summation network workstation (see Figure 17).

Law Firm administrators can limit case access to any subset of cases—one, some, or all of the Summation network cases can be exposed to the WebBlaze user.

In addition, different users can be given access to different portions of the case (see Figure 18).

Figure 16. The WebBlaze login screen.

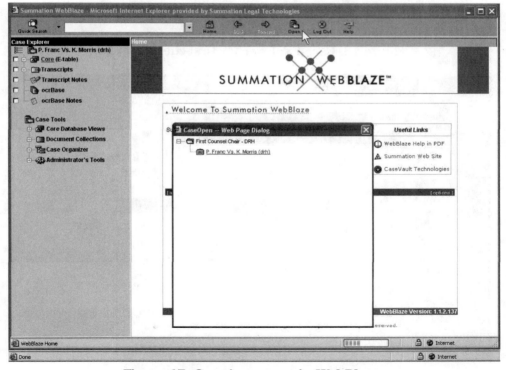

Figure 17. Opening a case in WebBlaze.

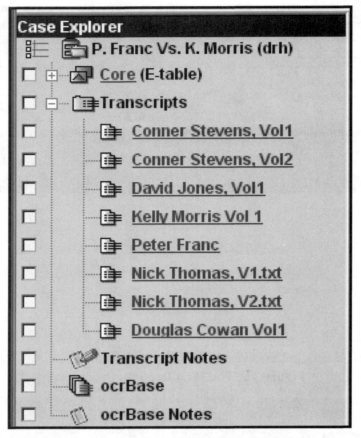

Figure 18. Case Explorer for first-chair lawyer.

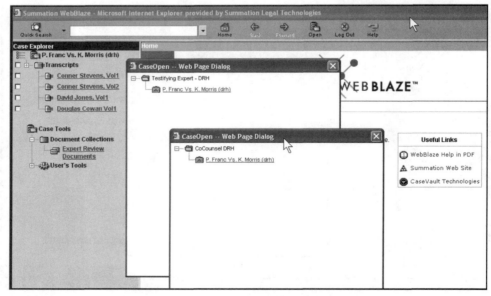

Figure 19. Custom WebBlaze case list.

Each WebBlaze user is assigned his or her own case list. In addition, Case Explorer elements can be limited for each user's status and contribution to the case. For example, testifying expert witnesses can be exposed to very limited collections of documents and transcripts, as well as limited information about those documents and transcripts to preserve privileges (see Figure 19).

Transcripts and Notes in WebBlaze

Working with transcript testimony and notes is very similar between LG/iBlaze and WebBlaze. Compare this view with that in Figure 6 in Chapter 3.

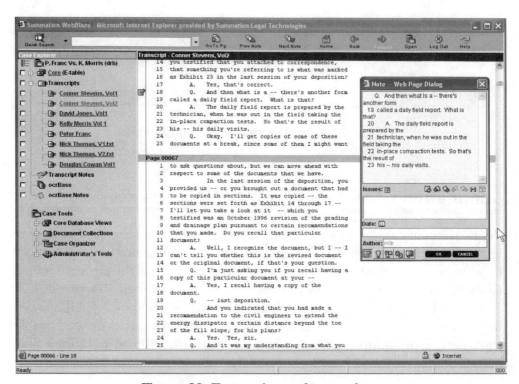

Figure 20. Transcript and note view.

Documents in WebBlaze

Working with documents is also very similar. You have access to the Core Database, images, full-text, and the like, from the same familiar desktop (see Figure 21).

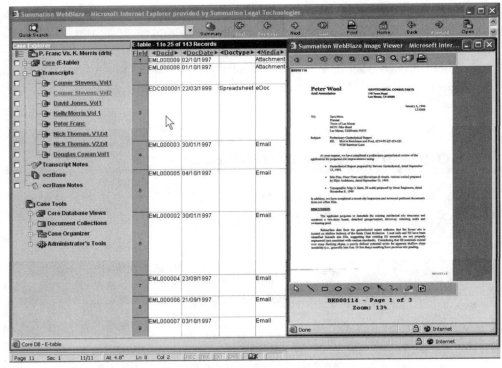

Figure 21. Core Database and image view.

Summation's CaseVault ASP Hosting Service

There are many reasons firms use an extranet to extend case data to lawyers and litigation team members, client counsel and representatives, co-counsel, experts and consultants, and the like. WebBlaze provides the perfect medium to extend the Summation system investment out through the World Wide Web. But there are many other reasons why a firm would not, or perhaps cannot, internally host the information, such as lack of resources or technical infrastructure, or multiple adverse-party involvement. In those situations, Summation's CaseVault ASP hosting service fits right in.

The CaseVault Case Explorer

Again, lawyers and litigation team members familiar with Summation can immediately work in the CaseVault environment (see Figure 22). All they need is a computer with the Microsoft Internet Explorer browser software and CaseVault security login and password information for the case.

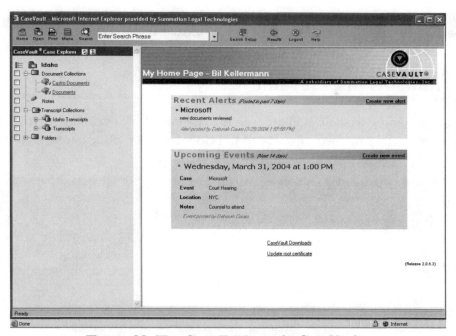

Figure 22. The Case Explorer in CaseVault.

Transcripts in CaseVault

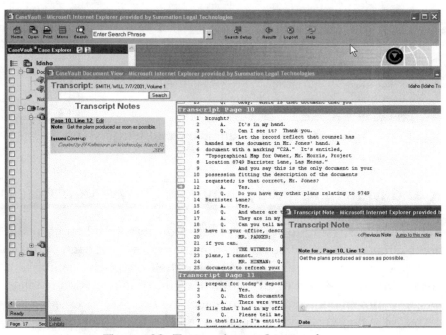

Figure 23. Transcript and note view.

Manage, search, review, and annotate the testimonial record of your case with the same workflow used in LG/iBlaze or WebBlaze (see Figure 23).

Documents in CaseVault

Manage, search, review, and analyze the documentary evidence in your case, again with the same workflow used in LG/iBlaze or WebBlaze (see Figure 24).

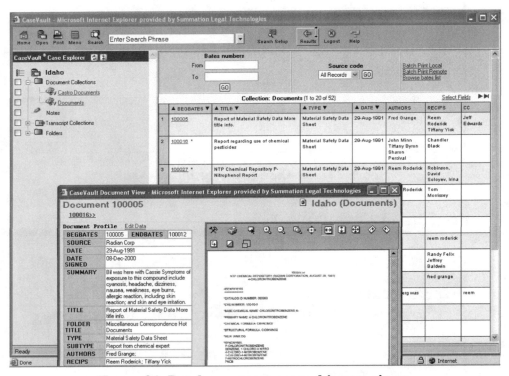

Figure 24. Database summary and image views.

Mix and Match: Anyway, Anyhow, Anywhere Access

The efficiency gains and lower total cost of ownership inherent in the Summation system should now be readily apparent. However, each of the components, while providing a tremendous tool in their own right, can be linked together to provide the best of all worlds in terms of information management, access, and movement from place to place.

The following section highlights several of the opportunities for interconnecting between information sources for a truly integrated access to your case anyway, anyhow, and anywhere you choose. These examples are representative, but not exclusive as to how the Summation system can be configured or extended to meet specific case needs.

Scenario 1: Creating a Case Information Intranet

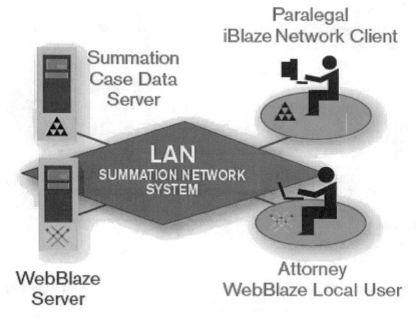

Figure 25. WebBlaze added on to an existing Summation iBlaze LAN system.

Scenario 2: Creating a Case Information Extranet

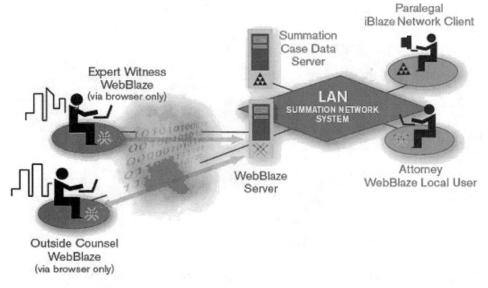

Figure 26. WebBlaze added on to an existing Summation iBlaze LAN system.

Scenario 3: Creating a Firm-Hosted Case Information Extranet

Figure 27. WebBlaze + iBlaze Mobile added on to an existing Summation iBlaze LAN system.

Scenario 4: Creating a Third-Party Hosted Case Information Extranet

Figure 28. Browser-only with iBlaze Mobile access to CaseVault hosted case data.

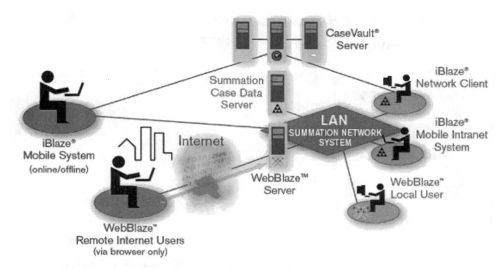

Figure 29. Integrated architecture for anyway, anyhow, anywhere access.

CaseVault Documents and Transcripts in iBlaze

Links to collections of documents or transcripts hosted on CaseVault, called CVDs and CVTs respectively, can be created or dropped into the iBlaze Case

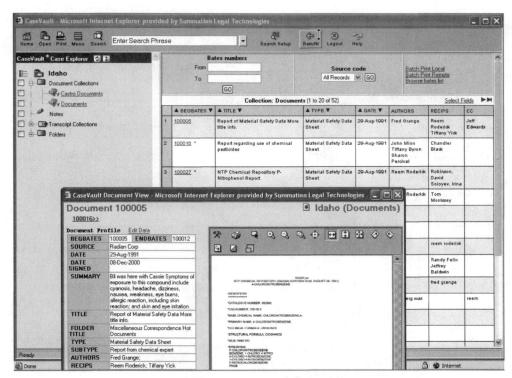

Figure 30. E-mailing the CVD link file.

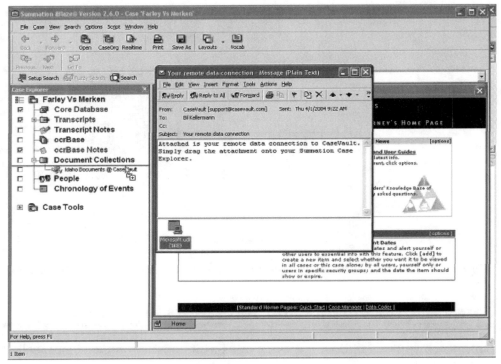

Figure 31. Dragging and dropping the link into Summation.

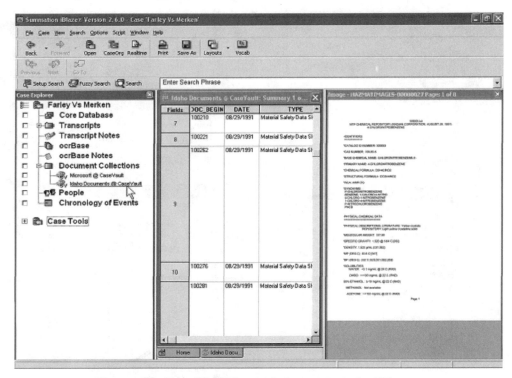

Figure 32. CaseVault hosted documents in iBlaze.

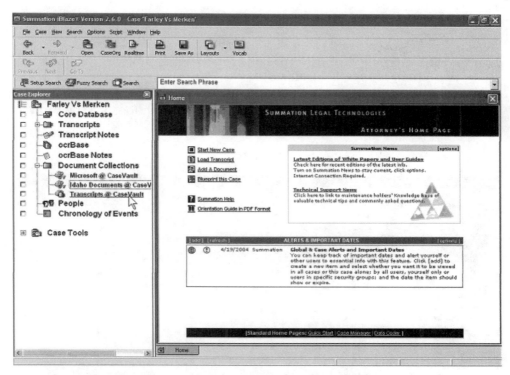

Figure 33. The CaseVault Transcript link (CVT) in iBlaze.

Explorer. Once the link is made available in the Case Explorer, iBlaze users can access, search, analyze, and manage information hosted on CaseVault. This gives the iBlaze user an inherent advantage over others who are limited to the CaseVault Web browser interface—offline access to the information via Briefcasing. The following section highlights those features.

As with Documents hosted on CaseVault, transcript collections are just as readily accessible. Transcripts can be searched remotely, and any transcript of interest can be quickly downloaded to the iBlaze case.

Briefcasing Document Information

As part of the dedication to a seamlessly integrated architecture, Summation developed an elegant currency by which to exchange information, the Summation Briefcase. Also known as the SBF, the Briefcase allows the iBlaze user to

- ◆ Capture online information hosted on a CaseVault or WebBlaze case for use offline
- ◆ Capture iBlaze case subsets for hosted use on CaseVault or exposure via WebBlaze

- ◆ Capture and preserve probative document collection subsets for future review
- ◆ Capture documents produced at deposition and load them in tandem with their respective transcript
- ◆ Capture collections of documents for production
- ◆ Create software-agnostic document review collections via the Browser Briefcase

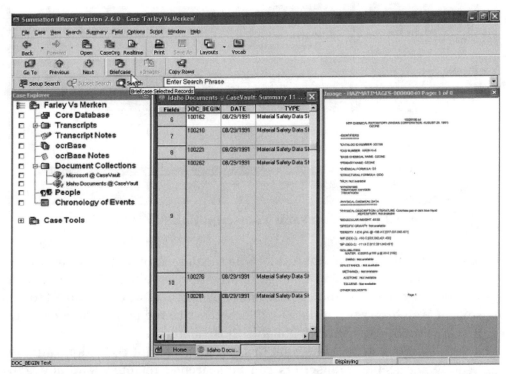

Figure 34. Access Imaged Documents and Associated Summaries Remotely Over the Internet.

Briefcases can be used in a similar fashion from any database for which access is granted in the iBlaze Case Explorer. Once the Briefcase is created, the information can be promoted to an existing Core Database using the Copy Rows feature. The Briefcase can also be exported out of the system for use in another Summation system. Last, the Briefcase can be exported as a Browser Briefcase for stand-alone review in the Internet Explorer browser.

Briefcase summary information along with related evidence in image, full-text, or native file formats can be exported with a right-click on the Briefcase folder. For Summation systems, formats include CaseVault compatible and Summation Briefcase Format (SBF). In addition, the Briefcase can be revealed to other users via WebBlaze.

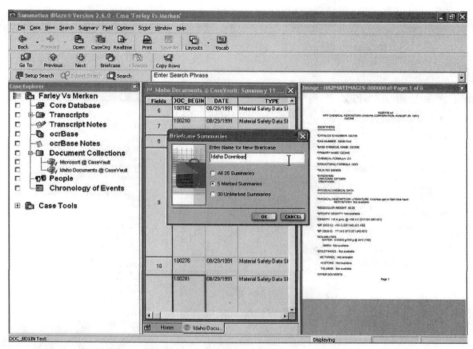

Figure 35. Use the iBlaze Briefcase function to Download Imaged Documents & Summaries of Interest.

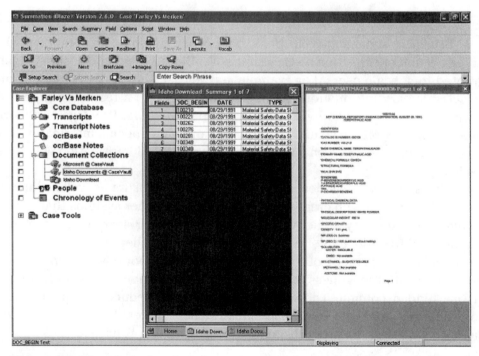

Figure 36. Five downloaded documents and associated summaries are now available anytime from the iBlaze version of the case.

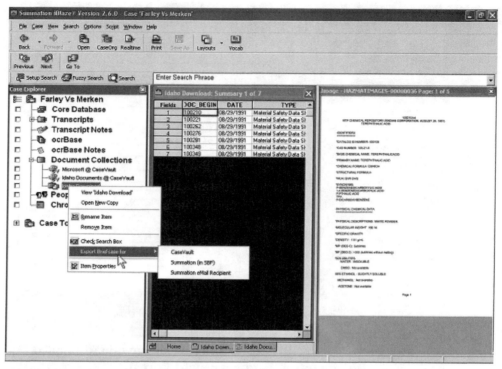

Figure 37. Exporting the Briefcase for other Summation systems.

Briefcase document collections can be viewed alone, or in tandem with other document collections based on the WebBlaze access and security rights granted to specific users. For example, a Briefcase subset of documents and select summary information can be revealed alone to a testifying expert allowing complete control over what that expert reviews. Privilege and work-product protection are insured—by carving out very specific information and preserving it, there is no chance privilege or protected information will be revealed.

This security precludes inadvertent direct disclosure as well as inferential disclosure based on creative search strategies. Other systems that rely on column level security alone, yet that use an index for search enhancement, can be used to deduce information by inference. In other words, a search for a witness reveals, among others, documents that do not readily appear to be associated with the witness, but for the fact that the name appears in an otherwise hidden column. The searcher can thereby deduce the document is somehow related to the witness in a way the host prefers to keep secret. This cannot happen with a properly configured Summation Briefcase.

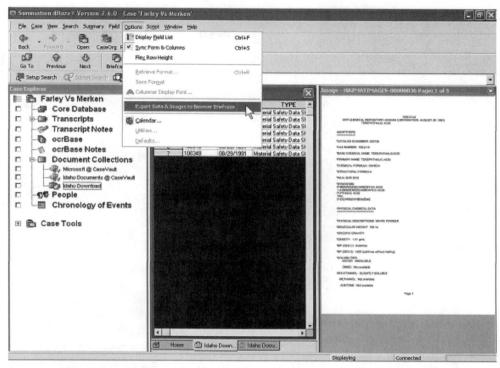

Figure 38. Exporting a Briefcase to the Browser Briefcase.

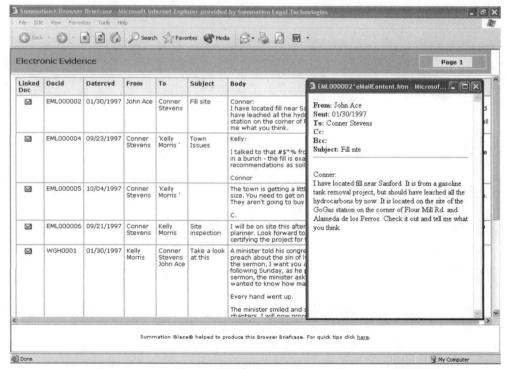

Figure 39. The Browser Briefcase exported from Summation.

Index

The Lawyer's Guide to Adobe® Acrobat®
by David L. Masters
This book will show you the power of using the Adobe Acrobat system and how to utilize its full potential in your law practice. Author David Masters takes readers step by step through the processes of creating then working with PDF documents. In subsequent chapters, Masters covers adding document navigation aids, commenting tools, using digital signatures, extracting content from PDF documents, searching and indexing, document security, saving Web pages to PDF, plug-ins, display mode, e-briefs, using Acrobat in the paperless office, and more.

The Lawyer's Guide to
Fact Finding on the Internet,
Second Edition
By Carole A. Levitt and Mark E. Rosch
Written especially for legal professionals, this revised and expanded edition is a complete hands-on guide to the best sites, secrets, and shortcuts for conducting efficient research on the Web. Containing over 600 pages of information, with over 100 screen shots of specific Web sites, this resource is filled with practical tips and advice on using specific sites, alerting readers to quirks or hard-to-find information. What's more, user-friendly icons immediately identify free sites, free-with-registration sites, and pay sites. An accompanying CD-ROM includes the links contained in the book, indexed, so you can easily navigate to these cream-of-the-crop Web sites without typing URLs into your browser.

Subscribe to *The Lawyer's Guide to Internet Fact Finding* E-Newsletter to stay current on the most valuable Web sites!
Each issue contains ten sites specifically chosen for their usefulness to legal professionals. Simply the best way to stay on top of Web sites that are important to you.

Persuasive Computer Presentations:
The Essential Guide for Lawyers
By Ann E. Brenden and John D. Goodhue
This book explains the advantages of computer presentation resources, how to use them, what they can do, and the legal issues involved in their use. It covers how to use computer presentations in the courtroom, during opening statements, direct examination, cross examination, closing arguments, and appellate arguments. It also covers using computer presentations outside the courtroom, during meetings, pretrial, and seminars. An accompanying CD-ROM is included with Corel Presentations® software and sample presentations used by lawyers to win big cases.

The Lawyer's Guide to Palm Powered™ Handhelds
By Margaret Spencer Dixon
The Palm-powered handheld is now an essential part of everyday life for an increasing number of lawyers. Whether you are a beginner, an advanced user, or simply deciding whether a Palm® PDA is right for you, this book will show you how a Palm-powered handheld can make you more efficient and effective at what you do. Written by a lawyer for lawyers, this guidebook provides helpful tips and tricks for getting the most out of Palm applications. Learn to take full advantage of your Palm Powered™ handheld to manage addresses, appointments, expenses, and time; write memos; take notes; check e-mail; read books and documents; and much more. In addition, you'll find a wealth of suggested Web sites and handy tips from top legal power users. If you're a lawyer searching for a book to get you up and running on the Palm platform and help you become a Palm power-user, look no further!

The Lawyer's Guide to Extranets:
Breaking Down Walls, Building Client Connections
by Douglas Simpson and Mark Tamminga
An extranet can be a powerful tool that allows law firms to exchange information and build relationships with clients. This new book shows you why extranets are the next step in client interaction and communications, and how you can effectively implement an extranet in any type of firm. This book will take you step-by-step through the issues of implementing an extranet, and how to plan and build one. You'll get real-world extranet case studies, and learn from the successes and failures of those who have gone before. Help your firm get ahead of the emerging technologies curve and discover the benefits of adopting this new information tool.

The Lawyer's Guide to Marketing on the Internet,
Second Edition
By Gregory H. Siskind, Deborah McMurray, and Richard P. Klau
The Internet is a critical component of every law firm marketing strategy—no matter where you are, how large your firm is, or the areas in which you practice. Used effectively, a younger, smaller firm can present an image just as sophisticated and impressive as a larger and more established firm. You can reach potential new clients, in remote areas, at any time, for minimal cost. Learn the latest and most effective ways to create and implement a successful Internet marketing strategy for your firm, including what elements you need to consider and the options that are available to you now.

How to Start and Build a Law Practice, Platinum Fifth Edition

By Jay G Foonberg

This classic ABA bestseller—now completely updated—is the primary resource for starting your own firm. This acclaimed book covers all aspects of getting started, including finding clients, determining the right location, setting fees, buying office equipment, maintaining an ethical and responsible practice, maximizing available resources, upholding your standards, and marketing your practice, just to name a few. In addition, you'll find a business plan template, forms, checklists, sample letters, and much more. A must for any lawyer just starting out—or growing a solo practice.

Marketing Success Stories: Conversations with Leading Lawyers

Hollis Hatfield Weishar and Joyce K. Smiley

This practice-building resource is an insightful collection of anecdotes on successful and creative marketing techniques used by lawyers and marketing professionals in a variety of practice settings. Whether you work in a solo, mid-sized, or mega-firm, these stories of marketing strategies that paid off will inspire you to greater heights. In addition to dozens of first-hand accounts of success stories from practitioners, you won't want to miss the advice from in-house counsel who give candid feedback on how strategic marketing influences their decision to hire a specific firm. Readers will also learn how to make new contacts, gain more repeat business, increase their visibility within the community, and many other action steps to take.

Compensation Plans for Law Firms, Fourth Edition

Edited by James D. Cotterman, Altman Weil, Inc.

In this newly revised and updated fourth edition, you'll find complete and systematic guidance on how to establish workable plans for compensating partners and associates, as well as other contributors to the firm. Discover how to align your firm's compensation plans with your culture, business objectives, and market realities. The book features valuable data from leading legal consulting firm Altman Weil's annual and triennial surveys on law firm performance and compensation, retirement, and withdrawal and compensation systems. You'll see where your firm stands on salaries and bonuses, as well as benefit from detailed analyses of compensation plans for everyone in your firm.

 **LawPracticeManagementSection**
MARKETING • MANAGEMENT • TECHNOLOGY • FINANCE

Results-Oriented Financial Management: A Step-By-Step Guide to Law Firm Profitability, Second Edition

By John G. Iezzi, CPA

This hands-on, how-to book will assist managing partners, law firm managers, and law firm accountants by providing them with the budgeting and financial knowledge they need to need to make the critical decisions. Whether you're a financial novice or veteran manager, this book will help you examine every facet of your financial affairs from cash flow and budget creation to billing and compensation. Also included with the book are valuable financial models on CD-ROM, allowing you to compute profitability and determine budgets by inputting your own data.

Paralegals, Profitability, and the Future of Your Law Practice

By Arthur G. Greene and Therese A. Cannon

This is your essential guide to effectively integrating paralegals into your practice and expanding their roles to ensure your firm is successful in the next decade. If you're not currently using paralegals in your firm, authors Arthur G. Greene and Therese A. Cannon explain why you need paralegals and how to create a paralegal model for use in your firm—no matter what the size or structure. You'll learn how to recruit and hire top-notch paralegals the first time. If you are currently using paralegals, you'll learn how to make sure your paralegal program is structured properly, runs effectively, and continually contributes to your bottom line. Finally, eight valuable appendices provide resources, job descriptions, model guidelines, sample confidentiality agreements, sample performance evaluations, and performance appraisals. In addition, all the forms and guidelines contained the appendix are included on a CD-ROM for ease in implementation!

The Lawyer's Guide to Marketing Your Practice, Second Edition

Edited by James A. Durham and Deborah McMurray

This book is packed with practical ideas, innovative strategies, useful checklists, and sample marketing and action plans to help you implement a successful, multi-faceted, and profit-enhancing marketing plan for your firm. Organized into four sections, this illuminating resource covers: Developing Your Approach; Enhancing Your Image; Implementing Marketing Strategies and Maintaining Your Program. Appendix materials include an instructive primer on market research to inform you on research methodologies that support the marketing of legal services. The accompanying CD-ROM contains a wealth of checklists, plans, and other sample reports, questionnaires, and templates—all designed to make implementing your marketing strategy as easy as possible!

30-Day Risk-Free Order Form
Call Today! 1-800-285-2221
Monday–Friday, 7:30 AM – 5:30 PM, Central Time

Qty	Title	LPM Price	Regular Price	Total
_____	The Lawyer's Guide to Adobe Acrobat (5110512)	$49.95	$54.95	$_____
_____	The Lawyer's Guide to Fact Finding on the Internet, Second Edition (5110497)	69.95	79.95	$_____
_____	The Lawyer's Guide to Fact Finding on the Internet E-mail Newsletter (5110498)	37.95	44.95	$_____
_____	Persuasive Computer Presentations: The Essential Guide for Lawyers (5110462)	69.95	79.95	$_____
_____	The Lawyer's Guide to Palm Powered™ Handhelds (5110505)	54.95	64.95	$_____
_____	The Lawyer's Guide to Extranets (5110494)	59.95	69.95	$_____
_____	The Lawyer's Guide to Marketing on the Internet, Second Edition (5110484)	69.95	79.95	$_____
_____	How to Start and Build a Law Practice, Platinum Fifth Edition (5110508)	57.95	69.95	$_____
_____	Marketing Success Stories: Conversations with Leading Lawyers, Second Edition (5110511)	64.95	74.95	$_____
_____	Compensation Plans for Law Firms, Fourth Edition (5110507)	79.95	94.95	$_____
_____	Results-Oriented Financial Management, Second Edition (5110493)	89.95	99.95	$_____
_____	Paralegals, Profitability, and the Future of Your Law Practice (5110491)	59.95	69.95	$_____
_____	The Lawyer's Guide to Marketing Your Practice, Second Edition (5110500)	79.95	89.95	$_____

*Postage and Handling	
$10.00 to $24.99	$5.95
$25.00 to $49.99	$9.95
$50.00 to $99.99	$12.95
$100.00 to $349.99	$17.95
$350 to $499.99	$24.95

**Tax
DC residents add 5.75%
IL residents add 8.75%
MD residents add 5%

*Postage and Handling	$_____
**Tax	$_____
TOTAL	$_____

PAYMENT

❑ Check enclosed (to the ABA)

❑ Visa   ❑ MasterCard   ❑ American Express

_____
Account Number   Exp. Date   Signature

Name _____ Firm _____

Address _____

City _____ State _____ Zip _____

Phone Number _____ E-Mail Address _____

Note: E-Mail address is required if ordering the
The Lawyer's Guide to Fact Finding on the Internet
E-mail Newsletter (5110498)

Guarantee
If—for any reason—you are not satisfied with your purchase, you may
return it within 30 days of receipt for a complete refund of the price of the
book(s). No questions asked!

Mail: ABA Publication Orders, P.O. Box 10892, Chicago, Illinois 60610-0892
♦ Phone: 1-800-285-2221 ♦ FAX: 312-988-5568

E-Mail: abasvcctr@abanet.org ♦ Internet: http://www.lawpractice.org/catalog

JOIN the ABA Law Practice Management Section (LPM) and receive significant discounts on future LPM book purchases! You'll also get direct access to marketing, management, technology, and finance tools that help lawyers and other professionals meet the demands of today's challenging legal environment.

Exclusive Membership Benefits Include:

- **Law Practice Magazine**
  Eight annual issues of our award-winning *Law Practice* magazine, full of insightful articles and practical tips on Marketing/Client Development, Practice Management, Legal Technology, and Finance.
- **ABA TECHSHOW®**
  Receive a $100 discount on ABA TECHSHOW, the world's largest legal technology conference!
- **LPM Book Discount**
  LPM has over eighty titles in print! Books topics cover the four core areas of law practice management – marketing, management, technology, and finance – as well as legal career issues.
- **Law Practice Today**
  LPM's unique web-based magazine in which the features change weekly! Law Practice Today covers all the hot topics in law practice management *today* – current issues, current challenges, current solutions.
- **Discounted CLE & Other Educational Opportunities**
  The Law Practice Management Section sponsors more than 100 educational sessions annually. LPM also offers other live programs, teleconferences and web cast seminars.
- **LawPractice.news**
  This monthly eUpdate brings information on Section news and activities, educational opportunities, and details on book releases and special offers.

Complete the membership application below.

Applicable Dues:
o$40 for ABA members   o$5 for ABA Law Student Division members

(ABA Membership is a prerequisite to membership in the Section. To join the ABA, call the Service Center at 1-800-285-2221.)

Method of Payment:
oBill me   Charge to my: oVisa   oMasterCard   oAmerican Express
Card number _____ Exp. Date _____
Signature _____ Date _____

Applicant's Information (please print):
Name _____ ABA I.D. number _____
Firm/Organization _____
Address _____ City/State/Zip _____
Telephone _____ FAX_____ Email _____

Fax your application to 312-988-5528 or join by phone: 1-800-285-2221, TDD 312-988-5168
Join online at www.lawpractice.org.

I understand that my membership dues include $16 for a basic subscription to *Law Practice Management* magazine. This subscription charge is not deductible from the dues and additional subscriptions are not available at this rate. Membership dues in the American Bar Association and its Sections are not deductible as charitable contributions for income tax purposes but may be deductible as a business expense.